PUBLISHED FOR THE MALONE SOCIETY
BY MANCHESTER UNIVERSITY PRESS

Oxford Road, Manchester, M13 9NR, UK
and Room 400, 175 Fifth Avenue, New York, NY 10010, USA
www.manchesteruniversitypress.co.uk

Distributed exclusively in the USA by
Palgrave, 175 Fifth Avenue, New York,
NY 10010, USA

Distributed exclusively in Canada by
UBC Press, University of British Columbia, 2029 West Mall,
Vancouver, BC, Canada V6T 1Z2

British Library Cataloguing-in-Publication Data
A catalogue record for this book is available from the British Library

Library of Congress Cataloging-in-Publication Data applied for

ISBN 978 0 7190 7709 8

First published 2007

Printed by Henry Ling Limited, at the Dorset Press, Dorchester, DT1 1HD

GUY OF WARWICK
1661

THE MALONE SOCIETY
REPRINTS, VOL. 170
2006

This edition of *Guy of Warwick* (1661) was prepared by Helen Moore, and checked by G. R. Proudfoot and H. R. Woudhuysen. The Society is grateful to the Provost and Fellows of Worcester College, Oxford, for permission to reproduce their copy of the book (Plays 4.64).

June 2006   H. R. WOUDHUYSEN

© *The Malone Society, 2007*

INTRODUCTION

Guy of Warwick was published in 1661 as *The Tragical History, Admirable Atchievments and various events of Guy Earl of Warwick* and was ascribed on its title-page to 'B. J.' It was printed for Thomas Vere (or Veere) and William Gilbertson (alias Derricke). Vere was among Gilbertson's pallbearers at his funeral in 1665, and during their working lives they were regularly associated in publishing ventures, particularly the publishing of ballads, in which both specialized. Indeed, their output is characterized by an interest in popular culture; in 1662, for example, *The Noble birth and gallant atchievements of that remarkable out-law, Robin Hood . . . newly collected into one volume by an ingenious antiquary* (Wing N1201) was printed for them. On 4 and 5 April 1655 Gilbertson had acquired a large number of copyrights of popular works from Edward Wright, including 'a Comedie of the Merry Deuill of Edmonton', 'The Tragicall history of King Leire, & his 3. Daughters', 'The Shooemakers Holiday or the Gentle Craft', 'The Tragicall history of ye horrible Life & death of D^r. Faustus', and 'The Comedy called Mucedorus'.[1] Although it is not named in the Stationers' Register, perhaps *Guy of Warwick* formed part of Gilbertson's acquisition from Edward Wright; certainly its pre-Civil War theatrical origins and associations with popular culture and Midlands folklore would have made it a natural choice for publication by Vere and Gilbertson.

The play figures in Kirkman's 1661 catalogue and was given an entry in Baker's *Biographia Dramatica*, where it is observed that:

The plot of this piece is founded on history, and it has been attributed to Ben Jonson; but we are apt to believe it only a conjecture formed from the letters prefixed to it, the execution of the work being greatly inferior to those of that first-rate genius.[2]

The play's subsequent critical reception has largely followed along these lines. It has excited interest for its potential links with Jonson and

---

[1] W. W. Greg, *A Bibliography of the English Printed Drama to the Restoration*, 4 vols. (London, 1939–59), i. 63; cf. G. E. B. Eyre and C. R. Rivington, *A Transcript of the Registers of the Worshipful Company of Stationers; From 1640–1708 A.D.*, 3 vols. (London, 1913–14), i. 469–71. For Gilbertson and Vere, see H. R. Plomer, *A Dictionary of the Booksellers and Printers who were at Work in England, Scotland and Ireland from 1641 to 1667* (London, 1907), pp. 82, 186.

[2] Greg, *Bibliography*, iii. 1344; David Erskine Baker, *Biographia Dramatica*, rev. Isaac Reed and Stephen Jones, 3 vols. in 4 (London, 1812), iii. 275–6.

Shakespeare, and is regarded as an interesting, if not artistically outstanding, example of romance drama. The play has never been edited, and has no attested stage history after 1660, although a Restoration revival seems to be the likely reason behind its printing in 1661.

The play collates 4°, A–F⁴ and contains twenty-four leaves. It is divided into five acts and is unpaginated. Nine copies are known to survive:

A	Abbotsford, by Melrose, Scotland, V.7 54
CHI	University of Chicago, Regenstein Library, PR3291.T77.1661
F	Folger Shakespeare Library, Washington, D.C., J5 cs79
HN	Huntington Library, San Marino, California, 152859 [−A1]
L	The British Library, 643.c.18
L⁶1	Victoria and Albert Museum Dyce Collection, D26 BOX 23.2 [−A2, A3]
L⁶2	Victoria and Albert Museum Dyce Collection, D26 BOX 23.3
O	Bodleian Library, Oxford, Mal. 214(2)
O⁶	Worcester College, Oxford, Plays 4.64

Correspondence with the librarian of the Newberry Library reveals that, *pace* Wing, no copy is held there.³ All copies except HN and L⁶1 are complete. The Huntington Library catalogue notes that HN (the copy reproduced in Early English Books Online) is the Kemble-Devonshire copy of the play, collated by Kemble in 1798. The missing title-page of HN is supplied in pen and ink facsimile, and omits the commas after 'WARWICK' and 'Applaufe'. The three rules dividing the ascription, the motto, and the imprint are also omitted. Three leaves of CHI have suffered damage (A2, A3, and A4), and the lower edge of D1 is cropped. The missing leaves of L⁶1 (A2 and A3) are also provided in manuscript transcription, the

---

³ *The Tragical History of Guy Earl of Warwick* is listed in the following reference works: Donald Wing, *Short-Title Catalogue of Books printed in England, Scotland, Ireland, Wales, and British America and of English books printed in other Countries, 1641–1700*, 2nd edn., 4 vols. (New York, 1982–98), J5; Greg, *Bibliography*, ii. no. 818(*A*); Alfred Harbage, *Annals of English Drama, 975–1700*, 3rd edn., rev. S. Schoenbaum and Sylvia Stoler Wagonheim (London, 1989), p. 60; Gertrude L. Woodward and James G. McManaway, *A Check List of English Plays 1641–1700* (Chicago, Ill., 1945), no. 661; and Yoshiko Kawachi, *Calendar of English Renaissance Drama 1588–1642* (New York and London, 1986), p. 70. I am indebted to Martin Wiggins, Helen Cooper, H. R. Woudhuysen, Richard Proudfoot, Laurie Maguire, and Michael Clark for their comments on parts of this introduction.

accuracy of which is generally high, suggesting that the replacement leaves were copied directly from another copy of the play.[4]

L⁶1 is of particular interest because it has a prefixed printed leaf with an imprimatur dated 'April. 6. 1639.' which generated an erroneous belief in a 1639 printing of the play. As Greg demonstrated, however, this imprimatur is in fact the licence leaf from *The Bride* (1640).[5] Walter Scott's copy of the play, held at Abbotsford, contains interesting annotations and underlinings. Scott has inscribed his first and last names on either side of the first line of the title-page and the upper endpaper bears the comment:

This Play is Rarissimus.

From the initials on the title-page it has been ascribed to Ben Jonson which is as true as the averral of the Biog: Dramatica that the plot is founded on history whereby Mr Baker probably meant as fable.

Scott's belief in the Jonson ascription may explain why the spine of his copy of the play is stamped 'JONSON'S HIST. OF GUY EARL OF WARWICK 1661'. The following words in A are underlined in pencil: 'Unch' (TLN 364), 'an Ambry' (365), 'Bruis' (367), 'Collefodiums' (513), 'darraigne' (624), 'I have catcht a *Pogon*' (753), and 'great Hoſe' (1219). The erroneous variant reading in A of 'door' for 'poor' (TLN 1502), possibly the result of a turned letter, is noted with the underlining of 'd' and the correction 'p' inserted in the margin. A line in the left-hand margin alongside TLN 1585–9 marks the section summarizing Guy's legendary achievements. This marginal annotation and the underlinings point to Scott's interest in the antiquarian matter and archaic vocabulary of the play.

This facsimile reproduces the copy belonging to Worcester College, Oxford. It is bound with John Kirke's tragicomedy *The Seven Champions of Christendome* (1638), in which Guy features as the eldest son of St George.[6] It is not known when *Guy of Warwick* was acquired by Worcester College, but it may have belonged to one of the two significant eighteenth-century

---

[4] The following erroneous readings occur: A2ᵛ TLN 32 '*rennes*' for '*renues*', 38 '*subdu d*' for '*ſubdu'd*', 41 '*performes*' for '*performs*', 51, '*glory*' for '*ſtory*, 54 '*Earl*' for '*Earl*,' 58 '*Age.*' for '*Age*,' 62 '*Winchester,*' for '*Winchester.*', 63 '*Guy*' for '*Guy.*', 'Thoſe' for 'Theſe', 66 'heares' for 'beares'; A3ʳ TLN 91 '*Warwick*'s' for '*Warwicks*', 103 'hote' for 'here', 104 'preſently,' for 'preſently.'; A3ᵛ TLN 106 'When' for 'when', 'Soueraign' for 'Soueraign;', 111–12 '*Phillis*' for '*Phillis*', 119 'leaue' for 'leave', 120 'ſpeak,' for 'ſpeak;', 126 'gaue' for 'gave', 131 'seruice' for 'ſeruice', 135 'Saviour' for 'Saviours', 138 '*Saracens.*' for '*Saracens*,', 140 '*Mahomets*' for '*Mahomet,*'.

[5] Greg, *Bibliography*, ii. 916.

[6] Greg, *Bibliography*, ii. no. 545(*A*).

bequests of dramatic texts to the College—by George Clarke in 1736 and by the Provost, William Gower, in 1777. Gower's bequest included part of Gerard Langbaine's collection. In the 1920s, money raised from the sale of duplicate copies was spent on further purchases of dramatic texts printed after 1660.[7] The copy is in good condition, with only light smudging and one ink stain: A2^v is smudged at the head; a small ink stain is present on the outer edge of leaves A3^r–B2^v; A4^v is smudged in the top-right corner, and there is an area of spotting beneath the running title on F4^r.

The play is mainly printed in roman type (20 lines = 80 mm), with italic used for proper nouns including speech prefixes, for the designation of acts, and generally for marginal stage directions. Time's verse choruses at the beginning of each act and his verse epilogue are set in italic with roman for proper names. In the headings for acts (TLN 21, 250, 529, 812, 1090) a large italic type is used, but the stage direction 'Enter' is set in roman. The fount-size used for the heading to the Epilogue (TLN 1596) is smaller than these act headings, but the same size as that used for major entries. These occur at TLN 52–3, 187, 271, 446, 455–7, 553–4, 626, 693, 720, 871, 1104, 1195, 1338, 1386, 1417, 1527, 1558 and most correspond to putative scene divisions. Like the Epilogue they are centred, with blank lines above and below; up to the direction at TLN 446 on B4^r they are set in roman with proper names in italic, thereafter (with the exception of TLN 553–4 on C1^v) they are set in italic with proper names in roman. A slightly smaller fount is used for the centred stage directions on C4^r (TLN 716–19) and D1^v (TLN 843–4); the centred stage direction at TLN 956 on D3^r is set in the same size as the text of the play and has no blank lines above or below it. Time's exits at the end of his speeches are signalled in roman (B1^v, TLN 270, D1^v, 842, E1^r, 1103) or a mixture of roman and italic (A2^v, 51, F4^r, 1611); there is no stage direction for his exit at the end of his speech (C1^v, 552) which begins the third act.

The type area of the pages measures approximately 148–150 mm × 98 mm. There are generally 38 lines of text per page, except where the use of a larger fount for stage directions reduces the number of lines to typically 34 or 35 (as, for example, on A2^v). There are variations in the type-depths of some pages. On three occasions pages were made short to allow a new act or scene to begin on a new page: so B1^r at the end of Act I has 35 lines, E2^r has 34 lines, and F3^v before Time's Epilogue has 36 lines (including a blank one)—this last page is preceded by a long one of 41 lines on F3^r. The last pages of gatherings A and

---

[7] [C. H. Wilkinson], *A Handlist of English Plays and Masques Printed before 1750 in the Library of Worcester College, Oxford* (Oxford, 1929), p. 3.

C are also short with 37 lines, suggesting errors in the casting off of copy. Although C4^v is a short page it also has an inserted stage direction, set in its own compartment, perhaps consisting of a quotation quadrat, to the left of the justified lines of Sparrow's prose speech in TLN 763–7. The stage direction is set in the small type found elsewhere only on D3^r and would appear to have been used in both instances to save space in a crowded page. Problems with casting off continued throughout gathering D in which the compositor found himself with too much material to set. It seems likely he began by setting the inner forme: on D1^v he lengthened the page depth by one line and when he turned to the outer forme he increased D2^v by two lines to 40 lines. He still had too much material to accommodate and on D3^r in the outer forme he resorted to a smaller size of fount for TLN 957–76 and had to produce a deeper than average page.

    The first two leaves of each gathering are signed, with the exception of A1, the title-page. On the three occasions when pages were set short before new acts or scenes (B1^r, E2^r, F3^v) signatures and catchwords in the direction line are set in the large fount also used for the running-titles and major centred stage directions: this does not occur on D4^v which contains 38 lines and has the catchword '*Actus*' set in the normal-size fount. There is no direction line on two of the longer pages, D3^r and F3^r, where the catchwords are set at the far right of the last lines of text. There are four minor instances of variation between the catchword and the first word on the next page.[8]

    An analysis of the running-titles on the basis of distinctive letters, textual variation, and measurements suggests the fairly regular use of two skeletons, one for the inner and the other for the outer formes. Sheets A and E employ the running-title '*The Tragicall Hiſtory | of* Guy *Earl of* Warwick.'. On the inner forme of sheets B, C, and D, however (B4^r, C4^r, and D4^r), the running-title omits the first '*of*' and the second is set in roman type, so giving '| Guy *Earl* of Warwick.'. The outer forme of sheet F also contains an anomalous unligatured -*ll*- in '*Tragicall*' on F2^v and a turned letter in 'Gny' in the running-title on F3^r. Other evidence includes the distinctive -*ſt*- ligature in '*Hiſtory*' on B–F1^v, a damaged *f* in the second '*of*' on B–E3^r and F2^r, as well as the double spacing after the second '*of*' on B–E2^r and F4^r. Measurements of running-titles suggest some further groupings (B–D2^v and E3^v; A2^v, B4^v, and C1^v; A4^v, B3^v, and C2^r, 4^r; B4^r, D4^r, and F1^r), with anomalous settings on A3^v, F2^v, and F3^r. Four settings of the recto running-title and four of the verso tended to recur in the same position in

---

   [8] See D1^v/D2^r (but/But), E2^v/E3^r (*Spar.*/*Sparrow.*), E4^v/F1^r (And/and), F3^v/F4^r (*Enter/* Enter).

B–D with some shifts in E and F, and two new settings in F (F2^v–3^r). These new settings in F may suggest the imposition of its inner forme before completion of the distribution of type from either forme of E. This use of running-titles implies that the printing of the quarto was a fairly orderly and efficient operation. The alternation of skeletons would have made for minimum loss of time at press.

Collation of the nine known copies has revealed variants in five of the twelve formes, with a significant number concentrated in sheet F:

Sheet B (inner forme)
B2^r 309   he rup . . . theConfidence] HN, L^{6}2
                            herup . . . the Confidence] ALL OTHER COPIES

Sheet D (outer forme)
D2^v 900, 902, 933
                            ſleep . . . Hercules , . . . ſh o uld] O
                            ſleep. . . . Hercules ; . . . ſhould] ALL OTHER COPIES
D3^r 948, 949, 953, 966
                            Glads . . . Livery, . . . of a curliſh . . . here] O
                            glad's . . . Livery! . . . of a churliſh . . . hear] ALL OTHER COPIES
D4^v 1060, 1075   and . . . makers] O
                            an . . . Makers] ALL OTHER COPIES

Sheet E (inner forme)
E3^v 1300   Life .] A
                            Life ;] ALL OTHER COPIES

Sheet F (outer forme)
F1^r 1385, 1392, 1392-3, 1398
                            Pilprimage . . . ca,me . . . preſent- | ly . . . great a] A, HN, L^{6}2
                            Pilgrimage . . . came . . . preſent- | ly, . . . a great] ALL OTHER COPIES
F2^v 1502
                            door] A, HN, L^{6}2
                            poor] ALL OTHER COPIES

Sheet F (inner forme)
F1^v 1438, 1441   Mire . . . maker] HN, L^{6}2
                            mire . . . Maker] ALL OTHER COPIES
F2^r 1455, 1468, 1479
                            Herod . . . live, . . . certainty ,] HN, L^{6}2
                            Herod, . . . live ; . . . certainty ;] ALL OTHER COPIES

F3ᵛ 1579   prevail,] HN, L⁶2
                  prevail] ALL OTHER COPIES
F4ʳ 1604, 1605
                  was . . . not,] HN, L⁶2
                  was, . . . not] ALL OTHER COPIES

The precise differentiation of the states of the inner forme of sheet E presents some difficulties. Apparent variant punctuation at two places in A and o probably results merely from failure of full points after '*Rain*' (1275) and '*you*' (1291) to impress in most copies.

Type shortages affected the setting of *Guy*, with the initial upper-case italic letters *G*, *H*, *P*, and *S* in names, speech prefixes, stage directions and catchwords being replaced by initial upper-case roman letters. Both roman and italic upper-case *W* is sometimes replaced by *VV*. Evidence of such shortages can be found in every forme in the quarto and is particularly marked in outer B and C; it is least evident in inner A and in both formes of D and F. The outer formes of all gatherings show more shortages overall than the inner ones, except in E where there are greater shortages in the inner than the outer forme and in F where the formes have identical shortages. The evidence would tend to suggest that the outer formes of gatherings B and C were probably set before the inner formes and that the inner forme of F was set before the outer: this last conclusion is supported by the running-title evidence discussed above. An anomalous initial italic upper-case *C* in 'Christ' on C4ᵛ (TLN 774) was probably caused by foul case.

There is considerable variation in the setting of the abbreviated form of 'I will', which occurs in four different guises.⁹ The distribution of forms is so random as to suggest that this is not evidence for more than one compositor at work on the text. The two least-used forms, 'il'e' and 'Ile' do not occur after B2ʳ; the predominant forms 'I'le' and 'i'le' are mixed randomly in the formes.

The play's stage directions are straightforward, detailing entrances, exits, and significant moments, such as '*Guy kneeleth.*' (B2ᵛ, TLN 351), '*Guy*

---

⁹ The forms are: I. 'il'e': A3ʳ (TLN 69); II. 'Ile': A4ᵛ (194); B1ʳ (225, 249); B2ʳ (293); III. 'I'le': B1ʳ (246); B3ᵛ (418); B4ᵛ (482, 499); C1ʳ (511); C2ʳ (573, 598); C3ʳ (649, 675); C4ʳ (745); C4ᵛ (759–62, 764–5); D1ʳ (796, 803); D2ʳ (892); D3ʳ (944, 946–7); D3ᵛ (997); D4ʳ (1031); D4ᵛ (1084, 1086); E1ᵛ (1125, 1155); E2ʳ (1190); E2ᵛ (1220); E3ᵛ (1288–90); E4ʳ (1323, 1332); E4ᵛ (1379); F1ʳ (1381); F2ᵛ (1491, 1506); F3ᵛ (1548); IV. 'i'le': B3ʳ (380); B3ᵛ (407); B4ᵛ (502); C1ʳ (510, 522); C4ʳ (749); D1ʳ (805); D3ᵛ (987); D4ʳ (1057, 1066, 1068, 1080); E2ʳ (1192); E3ᵛ (1269, 1294–5); E4ʳ (1312, 1331); E4ᵛ (1348); F1ʳ (1414); F1ᵛ (1415).

weeps.' (D4ʳ, 1051), or '*Guy groans.*' (F2ʳ, 1481). Particularly detailed directions are provided in the fairy scene of Act II, which features music and dancing (B4ʳ, TLN 455–7), thunder and lightning (B4ᵛ, 484), and the fairy pinching of Guy (C1ʳ, 503–4). Greater detail is also provided during the disguised encounter between Guy and Athelstone (D2ʳ⁻ᵛ, TLN 871, 887, 889, 899–900, 911) and the identification of Guy's body by his widow and son (F3ʳ, 1538–9). A sound effect is called for near the start of Act III, when a parley is signalled (C2ʳ, TLN 585). Alarums are sounded towards the end of the act (C3ᵛ, C4ʳ, TLN 693 and 717). Sparrow is occasionally given directions that indicate his state of mind or deportment, such as '*running*' (B4ᵛ, TLN 485) and '*crying*' (C3ʳ, 644), and in typical ranting fashion, the Sultan '*stamps*' at 748 (C4ʳ). The direction '*He Hollowes in his Ear.*' (E2ᵛ, TLN 1222) gives an insight into the playing of the comic encounter between Sparrow and Guy's son Rainborne in Act V. A small number of properties is called for. One, a halter or perhaps a noose (C4ʳ, TLN 751), is employed by Sparrow to bind a pagan. The required comic stage business concerning this halter, in which Sparrow is tricked by his captive, is detailed at TLN 763+(1–5) (C4ᵛ). At TLN 1126 (E1ᵛ) it is specified that a servant enters with bread and wine. The directions further reveal two staging requirements—walls for Jerusalem (C2ʳ, TLN 586) and a cave for Guy (F1ᵛ, 1417). Both are standard theatrical settings. Guy's cave is typical of the simple dwelling that featured in open country scenes, and the walls of a besieged city commonly provided the backdrop for military action.[10] The straightforward settings and small number of properties perhaps suggest a link between the 1661 quarto and an earlier touring production, a suggestion also advanced by Helen Cooper in relation to the quarto's short length.[11] Similarly, the occasionally detailed recording of stage business, as in the case of Sparrow and the halter, or his 'hollowing' in Rainborne's ear, may constitute a record of a particular actor's interpretation of the role of Sparrow. One possible scenario, then, is that the printer's manuscript derived from a touring company's prompt book.

Speech prefixes are indented, italic (with the exception of the initial roman capitals resulting from shortages of italic type), and end with a full point. Names are given in full until TLN 118 (A3ᵛ), which begins '*Phill.*' to accommodate a long line. Subsequently, abbreviated speech prefixes are the

---

[10] E. K. Chambers, *The Elizabethan Stage*, 4 vols. (Oxford, 1923), iii. 51, 54.
[11] Helen Cooper, 'Guy of Warwick, Upstart Crows and Mounting Sparrows', in *Shakespeare, Marlowe, Jonson: New Directions in Biography*, ed. Takashi Kozuka and J. R. Mulryne (Aldershot, 2006), p. 123.

norm. The first entry of Philip Sparrow is at TLN 187 (A4^v) where he is designated '*Clown*', which is then abbreviated to '*Clow.*' as a speech prefix. From his entry at TLN 271 (B1^v) he is designated '*Sparrow*', abbreviated to the speech prefix '*Spar.*', except at the beginning of his exchange with Rainborne (E2^v–3^r, TLN 1223–44), where both names appear in the speech prefixes in full (as does '*Sparrow*' at the beginning of his soliloquy (F1^r, 1387)). Perhaps this shift in designation, like the recording of Sparrow's comic business, indicates that the playing of Sparrow's part came increasingly to dominate the play in performance. At TLN 564 (C1^v), a speech prefix for Zorastes is lacking; this is supplied in brown ink in the margin in L^{6}1 as 'Zo' and in A in pencil as 'Zorast'. A superfluous speech prefix occurs at TLN 69 (A3^r), when '*Guy.*' is repeated in the middle of one of his speeches.

The play is composed primarily in iambic pentameter. The initial letter of each line is not normally capitalized: exceptions are Time's prologue to Act II (TLN 251–70) and the Epilogue (1597–1611). Prose is used for the comic scenes focused on Sparrow, breaking into verse for dramatic effect as in the case of his mock-heroics at TLN 333–8.

*

Two questions have dominated the study of *Guy of Warwick*, namely when was it written, and by whom? The earliest reference to a performance of a play of *Guy* occurs in John Taylor's account of his return from Scotland in 1618:

The next day I came to *London*, and obscurely comming within Moore-gate, I went to a house and borrowed money: And so I stole backe againe to *Islington*, to the signe of the Mayden-head, staying till Wednesday that my friendes came to meete mee, who knewe no other, but that Wednesday was my first comming: where with all loue I was entertained with much good cheere: and after Supper wee had a play of the life and death of *Guy of Warwicke*, plaied by the Right Honourable the Earle of *Darbie* his men. And so on the Thursday morning beeing the fifteenth of October, I came home to my house in *London*.[12]

A play on the subject of Guy, which may or may not be related to the one performed by the Earl of Derby's Men, was entered in the Stationers' Register to John Trundle on 15 January 1620:[13]

---

[12] John Taylor, *The Pennyles Pilgrimage* (London, 1618), G2^{r-v}.

[13] Greg, *Bibliography*, i. 31. Later, at ii. 916, Greg follows Chambers, *Elizabethan Stage*, ii. 127, in identifying this entry with the 1618 play reported by John Taylor. Gerald Eades Bentley also concurs, *The Jacobean and Caroline Stage*, 7 vols. (Oxford, 1941–68), iii. 251 and v. 1348.

Entred for his copie vnder the handes of Mr Tauernor and both the wardens A Play Called the life and Death of Guy of Warwicke written by Iohn Day and Tho: Decker

In December that year, the rights were assigned to Thomas Langley:[14]

Assigned ouer vnto him by Iohn Trundle and by Consent of Mr Lownes warden all the right the said Iohn Trundle hath in theis two Copies following viz
The Play of Guy of warwicke

Opinion has divided on the subject of the relationship of the play entered in the Stationers' Register in 1620 and ascribed to Day and Dekker to the 1661 quarto. J. O. Halliwell-Phillipps thought they were 'probably' the same play, whereas A. H. Bullen, the editor of Day's works, dismissed this possibility on the grounds of what he perceived as the poor quality of the 1661 play: 'I doubt whether either of the authors, if they had tried, could have written so execrably.'[15]

The possibility that the play of *Guy* in fact originated in the Elizabethan period has long hovered over discussion of the 1661 quarto. To Bentley, for example, it seemed 'more likely to be an Elizabethan or early Jacobean play than a later Jacobean or Caroline one'.[16] He was influenced in part by R. S. Crane's view that all of the material used in the play was available in the sixteenth century.[17] An early date of *c*.1593 was postulated by Alfred Harbage in an article in the *Shakespeare Association Bulletin*.[18] The *Annals of English Drama* correspondingly gave the limits of the play as *c*.1590–*c*.1615 and tentatively identified the 1620 Day and Dekker *Guy* as a 'revision' of this putative 1593 play.[19] To complicate matters further, Harbage believed that the 1661 play represents this older play, rather than the 1620 Day and Dekker play; making it 'the extant original of a lost revision'.[20] Harbage's suggestion of 1593 derives from his sense that *Guy* is 'archaic

---

[14] Greg, *Bibliography*, i. 32.

[15] James O. Halliwell, *A Dictionary of Old English Plays* (London, 1860), 113; *The Works of John Day Reprinted from the Collected Edition by A. H. Bullen (1881) with an Introduction by Robin Jeffs* (London, 1963), p. 645.

[16] Bentley, *Jacobean and Caroline Stage*, v. 1348.

[17] Ronald S. Crane, 'The Vogue of *Guy of Warwick* from the Close of the Middle Ages to the Romantic Revival', *PMLA*, 30 (1915), 125–94, 162–5.

[18] Alfred Harbage, 'A Contemporary Attack upon Shakespeare?', *Shakespeare Association Bulletin*, 16 (1941), 42–9. This article was reprinted in a revised form as 'Sparrow from Stratford' in *Shakespeare Without Words and Other Essays* (Cambridge, Mass., 1972), pp. 143–52.

[19] Harbage, *Annals*, pp. 60, 114.   [20] Harbage, 'Sparrow from Stratford', p. 149.

even for 1620', and his conviction that, given the existence of the Henslowe *Huon of Bordeaux* and *Godfrey* plays of 1593–4, 'patriotism would forbid' that 'foreign knights' such as these should appear on stage whilst an English hero such as Guy was neglected.[21] Furthermore, Act II of the play is derived from the romance of *Huon of Bordeaux*, chapters 32–4, which would have made it suitable company for these plays on the stage.[22] In this regard, note should also be taken of the reference in Henslowe's *Diary* to a play of 'brandymer' or 'brandimer' performed in 1592; 'Brandimart' is another name for the giant Colbrond in *Guy of Warwick*, so this may constitute a reference to a play on a theme derived from or related to *Guy*.[23] The construction as well as the matter of the play is also old fashioned: in the revised version of his article, Harbage wrote that the play is 'constructed like the early biographical chronicles, such as Marlowe's *Doctor Faustus*, with the exploits of the hero regularly coupled with the drolleries of the hero's clownish servant, while a Chorus or Presenter (in this case "Time") narrates deeds not presented in the action'.[24] Helen Cooper has recently returned to the subject of the play's archaism, arguing that elements such as its naïve stagecraft, Marlovian diction and versification, and engagement with the Vestiarian controversy speak of the very early 1590s, or even the late 1580s.[25]

Apart from its archaic style and dramaturgy, evidence of the play's latent Elizabethanism has also been found by Harbage and Cooper in the person of Philip Sparrow, discussed by both as a potential lampoon on Shakespeare. The relevant passage, which is somewhat reminiscent of the 'upstart crow' jibe in *Greene's Groatsworth of Wit* (1592), occurs in Act V during Sparrow's encounter with Guy's son, Rainborne:

> *Rainborne*. Art thou a Christian? prethee where wer't born?
> *Sparrow*. Ifaith Sir I was born in *England* at *Stratford* upon *Aven* in *Warwickſhire*.
> *Rainborne*. Wer't born in *England*? what's thy name?

---

[21] Harbage, 'Contemporary Attack', 42–3.
[22] *The Boke of Duke Huon of Burdeux*, ed. S. L. Lee, Part I, EETS e.s. 40 (1882), pp. 96–109.
[23] *Henslowe's Diary*, ed. R. A. Foakes and R. T. Rickert, 2nd edn. (Cambridge, 2002), pp. 17, 18. I am grateful to Martin Wiggins for this point.
[24] Harbage, 'Sparrow from Stratford', p. 145.
[25] Helen Cooper, 'Did Shakespeare Play the Clown?', *TLS* 20 April 2001, 26–7, and 'Guy of Warwick', pp. 119–38, 123–8.

> *Sparrow.* Nay I have a fine finical name, I can tell ye, for my name is *Sparrow*; yet I am not no houſe *Sparrow*, nor no hedge *Sparrow*, nor no peaking *Sparrow*, nor no ſneaking *Sparrow*, but I am a high mounting lofty minded *Sparrow*, and that *P*a*rnell* knows well enough, and a good many more of the pretty Wenches of our Pariſh ifaith.
>
> (TLN 1225–35)

Also pertinent to this argument is Sparrow's description of himself as 'A bird of *Venus*, and a Cock of the Game' in Act II (TLN 334). Harbage toyed with the idea that this alludes to *Venus and Adonis*, which was first published in 1593, and Cooper went further in suggesting that Shakespeare may even have taken the part of Sparrow in the play. Much depends on the striking juxtaposition between Sparrow's lowly character and the designation of himself as 'high mounting', which may have a sexual innuendo, and 'lofty minded', but an explanation for this need not rest on the coded presence of Shakespeare. In both *Guy of Warwick* and the comparable romantic play *Tom a Lincoln*, which (as discussed below) also features a clown, called Rusticano, much is made by both masters and their servants of high-mindedness as a marker of heroic potential. Guy declares to King Athelstone, with a Marlovian flourish, that royal favour 'hath plum'd my thoughts with Eagle-flighted wings, | and beares my mounting minde as high as Heaven' (TLN 65–6), whilst Tom a Lincoln urges his shepherd confreres to 'be like my mounting spirit | wich prompts and tells me that I was not borne | to base designm^{ts}'.[26] Both Sparrow and Rusticano are comic mirrors to the aspirations and actions of the heroes, and so they display a typically parodic desire to 'mount' in the world as a consequence of their mock-heroics (see for example Rusticano's speech in *Tom a Lincoln*, TLN 287–301). Sparrows were traditionally named Philip, as in John Skelton's mock elegy *Phyllyp Sparrowe*, a convention invoked by Faulconbridge in his riposte 'Philip?—sparrow!' to Gurney's greeting of him as 'good Philip' in *King John*.[27] It is undoubtedly 'curious', as Honigmann remarks in his note to this line, that at I. i. 225 Faulconbridge should also have alluded to the legend of Guy, in his mocking description of his brother Robert as 'Colbrand the giant, that same mighty man?'.

---

[26] *Tom a Lincoln*, ed. G. R. Proudfoot, Malone Society Reprints (Oxford, 1992), TLN 220–2.

[27] *King John*, ed. E. A. J. Honigmann, The Arden Shakespeare (London, 1954), I. i. 231.

Philip Sparrow and his father Old Sparrow are clearly marked as dialect speakers, as is Rusticano, who hails from Lincolnshire, in *Tom a Lincoln*. There is little in the Sparrows' speech, however, to indicate a specifically Warwickshire dialect rather than a generalized ruralism. The Sparrows' dialect is essentially the literary southern dialect that was frequently used for comic purposes in early modern drama. The standard literary methods of depicting southern dialect are represented in their speech, for example in the voiced consonants [z] and [v] for [s] and [f] (hence 'son' and 'forty' are rendered as 'zoon' and 'vorty' respectively (TLN 197 (cf. 'foon' 238) and 200); in elided forms such as 'chill' for 'I will' or 'I'll' (207) and 'ha' for 'have' (244); in amalgamated forms such as 'quotha' (276) and 'wees me' for 'woe is me' (238–9); and in the use of 'che' (204), a variant of the southern first-person pronoun 'ich'. Sparrow's dialect vocabulary is broadly representative of the Midlands, whilst encompassing the occasional northernism such as 'Barne' (child, TLN 209), 'Ambry' (cupboard, 365), and 'Bruis' ('brewis', broth, 367). Typically Midlands words include 'Slops' (breeches, TLN 1409); 'Emmot' (the Northampton version of 'emmet', ant, 295); 'trundle' (attested in Lincolnshire as indicating a pregnant woman, 339); 'Snapfacks' ('snap' meaning a portion of food, 661); 'Snukering' ('snuck' meaning to smell, 1410) and 'edgling' ('edgelong' or edgeways, 1414).[28]

One important piece of evidence relating to performance and dating is found in Thomas Nabbes's *Covent Garden* (performed 1632), in which two country characters, Dobson and Ralph, discuss their arrival in Covent Garden:

> *Dobs.* Dost thinke we shall dwell hereabouts?
> *Ralph.* I hope so: we shall then be neere the *Cock-pit*, and see a Play now and then.
> *Dobs.* But tell me *Ralph*, are those Players the ragged fellowes that were at our house last *Christmas*, that borrowed the red blanket off my bed to make their Major a gowne; and had the great Pot-lid for *Guy* of *Warwicks* Buckler?[29]

---

[28] Joseph Wright, ed., *The English Dialect Dictionary*, 6 vols. (London, 1898–1905); Paula Blank, *Broken English: Dialects and the Politics of Language in Renaissance Writings* (London and New York, 1996); G. F. Northall, *A Warwickshire Word-Book*, English Dialect Society, 79 (London, 1896); Appleton Morgan, *Venus and Adonis. A Study in Warwickshire Dialect* (New York, 1885); Hilda Hulme, 'Shakespeare of Stratford', *Review of English Studies*, NS 10 (1959), 20–5.

[29] Thomas Nabbes, *Covent Garden: A Pleasant Comedie* (London, 1638), B1ᵛ.

Crane treated this as a definite reference to a country performance of the 1620 *Guy*, which is not necessarily what the passage implies.[30] As Bentley pointed out, 'the allusion is such that almost any kind of entertainment involving Guy of Warwick could be intended'.[31] Biographers of Shakespeare from John Aubrey onwards have noted that rural calf-killing stunts reminiscent of Guy's heroics may have formed part of the young playwright's dramatic initiation.[32]

Apart from the title-page reference to the play's having been 'Acted very Frequently with great Applaufe, | By his late MAJESTIES Servants', there is no record of *Guy*'s performance in the 1659–62 seasons that surrounded its publication.[33] Harbage's views on early dating led him to the trenchantly expressed opinion that this statement was 'invented for a title-page refurbishing an old book. It is extremely unlikely that any play of the type of *Guy of Warwick* was ever acted by the modish King's Company in the time of Charles or even in the time of James.'[34] Bentley was similarly sceptical about the likelihood of the play's performance, stating that 'The play published in 1661 is a crude piece which probably was never acted by the King's company, as the title-page says.'[35] However, such a play of Guy would have been very much of a piece with the repertory of the King's Men at the time: of the forty-three plays they acted in 1661 most were revivals. As Gunnar Sorelius has remarked, the King's Men were the 'custodians of dramatic heritage' because most of the older, pre-Civil War actors were

---

[30] Crane, 'Vogue', 161.

[31] Bentley, *Jacobean and Caroline Stage*, v. 1348. An unfortunate error has crept into the account of this allusion. Greg, *Bibliography*, ii. 916, states on the basis of this extract that a 'Guy of Warwick' play was performed at the Cockpit 'about Christmas 1631', whereas in fact the reference is to a country performance and there is an explicit contrast between the standing of the country and the Cockpit players. The mistake about a Cockpit performance is repeated for example in Velma Bourgeois Richmond, *The Legend of Guy of Warwick* (New York and London, 1996), p. 203.

[32] *'Brief Lives', Chiefly of Contemporaries Set Down by John Aubrey, Between the Years 1669 & 1696*, ed. Andrew Clark, 2 vols. (Oxford, 1898), ii. 226, reports Shakespeare's killing of a calf 'in a high style' and the tradition is discussed by Katherine Duncan-Jones in *Ungentle Shakespeare: Scenes from his Life* (London, 2001), p. 15.

[33] Ben Ross Schneider, *Index to 'The London Stage 1660–1800'* (Carbondale, Ill., 1979), p. 374.

[34] Harbage, 'Contemporary Attack', 42.

[35] Bentley, *Jacobean and Caroline Stage*, v. 1348.

included in that company; in this context, *Guy of Warwick* would not have seemed unduly out of place.³⁶

The title-page describes the play as 'Written by B. J.', but this is a spurious ascription, most probably intended to exploit the cultural capital of Jonson, who was pre-eminent amongst the Jacobean dramatists revived on the Restoration stage.³⁷ A straining after Jonsonian associations may also lie behind the use of the second line of a Martial epigram (I. 91) on the title-page. The full epigram reads

> Cum tua non edas, carpis mea carmina, Laeli.
> carpere vel noli nostra vel ede tua.³⁸

This epigram does not actually appear in any of Jonson's plays, but the theme of unhappy relations between readers and critics was a topos in Martial and Horace much exploited by Jonson. Martial's epigrams had, indeed, provided epigraphs for the quartos of *Poetaster* (1602) and *Sejanus* (1605).³⁹ The second half of this epigram had been used previously on the title-page of Thomas Jordan's comedy *The Walks of Islington and Hogsdon* (1657), printed by Thomas Wilson. On this title-page the quotation is located in the same position as on the title-page of *Guy*, under the authorial ascription ('Written by *Tho. Jordan*, Gent.'). *The Walks of Islington and Hogsdon* is in fact the published form of Jordan's second comedy, *Youths Figaries*, which was performed in 1641 at the Red Bull, the King's Company playhouse in Clerkenwell (where Jordan was himself an actor at the time). Like the title-page of *Guy*, it trumpets the success enjoyed by the play in performance: 'As it was publikely Acted 19. days toge-|ther, with extraordinary Applauſe'. Lynn Hulse has pointed out that a reference to the Quaker movement in *The Walks of Islington and Hogsdon* (E3ᵛ) suggests that

---

³⁶ Gunnar Sorelius, '*The Giant Race Before the Flood': Pre-Restoration Drama on the Stage and in the Criticism of the Restoration*, Acta Universitatis Upsaliensis, Studia Anglistica Upsaliensia, 4 (Uppsala, 1966), p. 40.

³⁷ Sorelius, '*Giant Race*', pp. 31, 78. Jesse Franklin Bradley and Joseph Quincy Adams, *The Jonson Allusion Book: A Collection of Allusions to Ben Jonson from 1597 to 1700*, Cornell Studies in English 45 (New Haven, CT, 1922), supplemented by C. B. Graham, 'Jonson Allusions in Restoration Comedy', *Review of English Studies*, 15 (1939), 200–4; Robert Gale Noyes, *Ben Jonson on the English Stage 1660–1776* (Cambridge, Mass., 1935).

³⁸ Martial, *Epigrams*, ed. and trans. D. R. Shackleton Bailey, 3 vols. (Cambridge, Mass., and London, 1993), i. 108–9: 'Although you don't publish your own poems, Laelius, you carp at mine. Either don't carp at mine or publish your own.'

³⁹ See Robert S. Miola, 'Creating the Author: Jonson's Latin Epigraphs', *Ben Jonson Journal*, 6 (1999), 35–48, and Michael Clark, 'In a Martial Hand: Studies in the Epigram in Early Modern Britain', unpublished D.Phil. thesis, University of Oxford (2002), ch. 5.

the play had been revised between performance in 1641 and publication in 1657. The unsold sheets of the play were reissued, with new preliminaries, in 1663 under the title *Tricks of Youth*, having been performed in 1661 or 1660.[40] The connections of Jordan's *Walks* with *Guy* are slight, but nonetheless suggestive: they both make use of the Martial epigram, and were revived at about the same time. Beyond this, there is a shared royalist association: Thomas Jordan was a well-known and vocal royalist in theatrical and City circles and, as discussed below, *Guy of Warwick* may have possessed a certain royalist appeal. The Martial tag may perhaps have served as a marker asserting renewed dramatic and political continuities by directing attention to the fact that both plays were revivals of earlier dramas, and defending the practice of revival against its critics. There is no record of a performance of *Guy* at the Red Bull in the years immediately preceding the Civil War, but it is conceivable that *Guy of Warwick* may have surfaced at the Restoration, perhaps even through the agency of Thomas Jordan. The play's ascription on its title-page to 'B. J.' may even conceivably be an error for 'T. J.', suggesting an association of some kind with Thomas Jordan.

Whilst the cultural capital of Jonson's plays is the most likely reason for the 'B. J.' attribution, it is worth pausing to consider the possibility that the ascription was made in recognition of the connections between *Guy* and a handful of works by Jonson. The most substantial of these links figures in *The Magnetic Lady* (performed in 1632), in which Jonson provides a comical summary of a romantic drama that is suggestive of a play of *Guy of Warwick*:

> *Boy*. . . . So, if a Child could be borne, in a *Play*, and grow up to a man, i'the first Scene, before hee went off the Stage: and then after to come forth a Squire, and bee made a Knight: and that Knight to travell betweene the Acts, and doe wonders i'the holy land, or else where; kill Paynims, wild Boores, dun Cowes, and other Monsters; beget him a reputation, and marry an Emperours Daughter for his Mistris; convert her Fathers Countrey; and at last come home, lame, and all to be laden with miracles.[41]

This summary need not, of course, refer to the surviving *Guy* or to any of its possible predecessors. There is, however, a section of *Guy* that is very close

---

[40] Lynn Hulse, 'Thomas Jordan', in *ODNB*.
[41] *The Magnetic Lady*, I, Chorus, 16–24 in *Ben Jonson*, ed. C. H. Herford, Percy Simpson and Evelyn Simpson, 11 vols. (Oxford, 1925–52), vi. 527–8. On the identification of this link, see Harvey W. Hewett-Thayer, 'Tieck and the Elizabethan Drama: his Marginalia', *Journal of English and Germanic Philology*, 34 (1935), 377–407, 402.

in wording to this description, and may suggest not only that Jonson lifted his comic summary from a play of *Guy of Warwick*, but also that the play printed in 1661 is a close relation of this play as it was performed:

> *Spar*. . . . my Miſtris P*arnell* is as precious to me, as
> your Lady P*hillis* is to you, we have gotten them both with child;
> and all the difference is, that P*hillis* is your wedded VVife, and
> P*arnell* is my unmarried Miſtris, and we muſt needs run up and
> down killing of Dun Cowes, Dragons, VVild-boars and Maſtiff
> Dogs, when we have more work at home then we can well turn
> our hands to.
>
> (TLN 340–6)

The folklore Guy also appears in Jonson's play *A Tale of a Tub* (performed in 1633), in which Guy of Warwick and Bevis of Hampton are listed as famous 'high Constables' (III. vi. 6–7). An indirect connection between Jonson and the play of *Guy* exists via *Huon of Bordeaux*, which was not only a source for *Guy* but a likely source for the name Oberon as borne by Prince Henry in Jonson's masque *Oberon, The Fairy Prince* (performed in 1611).[42] In chapter 32 of the romance, Huon is warned not to speak to Oberon, the fairy king, but does so anyway, and is rewarded with an ivory horn. He then disobeys the advice of Oberon in turn, in order to enter the tower of Donather and fight the giant, as recounted in Act II of the play:

> *Guy*. This is the ſtately Tower of *Donather*,
> where *Huon* of *Burdeaux* a couragious Knight
> flew *Angolofar* in a ſingle Fight:
>
> (TLN 387–9)

A third link resides in the superficial similarity in subject matter and delivery between *Guy* and Jonson's unfinished play, *The Sad Shepherd* (first printed in 1641). Like *Guy*, *The Sad Shepherd* draws its material from English folklore, a process that is likened by Jonson to his Muse's pulling wool '*from meere* English *Flocks*' (*Ben Jonson*, vii. 9). The sub-title of *The Sad Shepherd* is 'A Tale of *Robin-Hood*' and it features folklore stalwarts such as Robin and Maid Marian, Friar Tuck and Little John, the witch Mother Maudlin, and 'Puck-hairy', alias Robin Goodfellow. Furthermore, *The Sad Shepherd* is highly unusual amongst Jonson's plays in featuring northern English dialect. The huntsman Scathlock, Maudlin, and her daughter Douce are all at various points dialect speakers, although their use of dialect is inconsistent even within individual scenes (see in particular I. vi

---

[42] *Ben Jonson*, x. 526.

and II. vi for Scathlock and II. vi for Maudlin). This inconsistency prompted Herford and Simpson to ask 'Did Jonson first write in plain English and then work up his dialect?'; they go on to describe his treatment of dialect as 'amateurish' (*Ben Jonson*, x. 363). Perhaps as a consequence of the Oberon masque and *The Sad Shepherd*, Jonson became spuriously associated with the related tradition of fairy ballads; for example, the ballad entitled 'The mad-merry prankes of Robbin Good-fellow' ([1625]) that begins with the line 'From *Oberon* in Fairy Land', has sometimes been attributed to Jonson (*Ben Jonson*, viii. 426). Over and above these general similarities between *Guy* and Jonson's masque and play, however, there is nothing in the substance, style, or dramaturgy of *Guy of Warwick* to warrant the attribution of the play to Jonson.

Given this, attention must turn to the alternative candidate, Thomas Dekker, whose joint authorship with John Day of 'A Play Called the life and Death of Guy of Warwicke' is attested by the 1620 Stationers' Register entry. Dekker had been imprisoned for debt in the King's Bench prison from 1612 to 1619, and on his return to theatrical life he embarked on a series of dramatic revisions and collaborations. Several of these were staged at the Red Bull, such as his first play after his release, *Match Me in London*, which was played there in 1620, as was his collaboration with Massinger, *The Virgin Martyr*. Two collaborations with John Day were also staged at the Red Bull in the years following Dekker's release: *The Bellman of Paris* (1623) and *Come See a Wonder* (which may or may not be the same play as *The Wonder of a Kingdom*).[43]

Despite the many Restoration revivals of pre-Civil War plays, Dekker enjoyed only a slight reputation in the 1660s, and was implicitly contrasted with Jonson.[44] The 'B. J.' attribution would therefore be an unsurprising means of passing off a play by Dekker as by Jonson. Various elements of *Guy* may indicate Dekker's involvement, and may therefore suggest that the 1661 quarto is, after all, connected to the play ascribed to Day and Dekker in 1620. Harbage noted instances of stylistic traits linked to Dekker, such as iteration and the term 'Hell-hound' (TLN 422), as well as a handful of possible echoes from Dekker's plays.[45] There is some overlap between the diction of *Guy* and that of attested Dekker plays, although none of

---

[43] M. T. Jones-Davies, *Un Peintre de la Vie Londonienne: Thomas Dekker*, 2 vols. (Paris, 1958), i. 62 and ii. 401, 403–4.

[44] Larry S. Champion, *Thomas Dekker and the Traditions of English Drama* (New York, Berne, Frankfurt, 1985), p. 2, and Bentley, *Jacobean and Caroline Stage*, iii. 245.

[45] Harbage, 'Contemporary Attack', 44–5.

these similarities points conclusively towards Dekker's authorship. Two of Sparrow's favourite foods, bagpudding and brewis (TLN 366, 367), appear in *Satiromastix* (IV. iii. 151) and *The Shoemaker's Holiday* (I. iv. 2 and IV. i. 31), as do several other striking or unusual words from *Guy*, such as 'Shittlecock' (TLN 1394; *Satiromastix* III. i. 164), 'Slops' (TLN 1409; *Shoemaker's Holiday* I. i. 221), and 'twindge' (TLN 190; *Shoemaker's Holiday* I. iv. 34).[46] Perhaps most commandingly, *Guy* manifests Dekker's thoroughly attested interest in popular culture. *Guy of Warwick* was the best known of English popular romances, and in one attack upon the genre, Henry Crosse's *Vertues Common-wealth* (1603), Guy is linked with various figures of folklore and popular culture including Fortunatus, the subject of Dekker's play *Old Fortunatus* (performed in 1599):

> For if a view be had of these editions, the Court of *Venus*, the Pallace of Pleasure, *Guy* of *Warwicke*, *Libbius* and *Arthur*, *Beuis* of *Hampton*, the wise men of *Goatam*, *Scoggins* Ieasts, *Fortunatus*, and those new delights that haue succeeded these, and are now extant, too tedious to recken vp: what may we thinke? but that the floud-gates of all impietie are drawne vp, to bring a vniuersall deluge ouer all holy and godly conuersation . . .   (O1ᵛ–2ʳ)

There are two further links between *Guy* and *Old Fortunatus*: the name Athelstone, which figures in Dekker's *The Welsh Ambassador* (1624) as well, and the use of a chorus (Time, in the case of *Guy*) to summarize omitted action; Harbage observed that 'the device was already old-fashioned in 1599' when Dekker used it in *Old Fortunatus*.[47] Furthermore, the dramatic records of Sir Henry Herbert also record the licensing of a play called *The Fairy Knight* by Dekker and Ford in 1624. Chambers was dismissive of Fleay's identification (purely on the basis of the names) of this play with *Huon of Bordeaux*, revived by Sussex's men in December 1593. However, since *Huon* is the source for the Oberon elements of *Guy*, it is potentially significant that Dekker wrote a lost play that may have been a version of the Huon story.[48] There is also some similarity with *Patient Grissil* (entered in

---

[46] V. A. Small, R. P. Corballis, and J. M. Harding, eds., *A Concordance to the Dramatic Works of Thomas Dekker*, 5 vols., Salzburg Studies in English Literature, Jacobean Drama Studies, 82 (Salzburg, 1984). All references are to *The Dramatic Works of Thomas Dekker*, ed. Fredson Bowers, 4 vols. (Cambridge, 1953–61).

[47] Harbage, 'Sparrow from Stratford', p. 146.

[48] Chambers, *Elizabethan Stage*, iii. 304. An alternative possibility is that this play refers to the Fairy Knight who was the son of Tom a Lincoln and the Fairy Queen; see Muriel C. Bradbrook, 'A New Jacobean Play from the Inns of Court', *Shakespearean Research and Opportunities*, 7–8 (1972–4), 1–5, 4.

the Stationers' Register in 1600) in that it, like *Guy of Warwick*, mixes comedy with a testing theme.[49]

Certain connections with Dekker and Massinger's collaboration *The Virgin Martyr* (performed in 1620 and published in 1622) are worthy of note. The most striking is the title-page, which is alone amongst early Dekker editions in carrying very similar wording to that of *Guy of Warwick*.[50] *The Virgin Martyr* was 'reformed' and licensed for the Red Bull on 6 October 1620; it was then entered in the Stationers' Register to Thomas Jones on 7 December 1621 and printed by Bernard Alsop.[51] It was reprinted in 1631, 1651, and 1661, and was revived by the King's Men in 1661 and 1667, thus suggesting further similarities with *Guy*.[52] *The Virgin Martyr* is based upon the legends of Dorothea and Agnes which, whilst possessing obvious Catholic appeal, also appear in Foxe's *Actes and Monuments*.[53] Like *Guy*, *The Virgin Martyr* stages the practice of piety and is consciously archaic. It is also Dekker's only surviving tragedy.[54] Furthermore, *The Virgin Martyr* may be a revision of the play of *Diocletian*, listed by Henslowe as performed twice in November 1594, and as such it may offer a parallel for Day and Dekker's putative rewriting (if such it is) of an Elizabethan *Guy* play, which turned it into the play that was licensed in 1620.[55]

The likelihood of Dekker's co-authorship may have some bearing on the question of whether Sparrow may be a lampoon on Shakespeare. *The Shakspere Allusion-Book* is useful here: it identifies two Dekker references to Shakespeare, in *A Knight's Conjuring* (1607) and *The Dead Term* (1608). *The Allusion-Book* identified a further eleven works by Dekker which may borrow from, echo, or allude to Shakespeare's poems and plays. The highest concentration of allusions (three) comes, not surprisingly, in *Satiromastix* (1602).[56] Dekker was clearly not averse to writing Shakespeare into his plays, but the attribution of *Guy* to Dekker would neither specifically advance nor deny the likelihood of a Sparrow–Shakespeare link.

[49] As remarked by Champion, *Thomas Dekker*, p. 15.
[50] A. F. Allison, *Thomas Dekker: A Bibliographical Catalogue of the Early Editions (To the End of the 17th Century)* (Folkestone and London, 1972), no. 76 and plate 80.
[51] *Dramatic Works of Thomas Dekker*, iii. 367.
[52] Sorelius, '*Giant Race*', pp. 42–3, 54.
[53] Julia Gasper, 'The Sources of *The Virgin Martyr*', *Review of English Studies*, NS 42 (1991), 17–31.
[54] Champion, *Thomas Dekker*, pp. 105–6, 115.
[55] *Henslowe's Diary*, p. 25, and Harbage, 'Sparrow from Stratford', p. 149.
[56] John Munro, *The Shakspere Allusion-Book: A Collection of Allusions to Shakspere from 1591 to 1700*, rev. E. K. Chambers, 2 vols. (London, 1932).

Of course, the *Guy of Warwick* licensed in 1620 was attributed to Day and Dekker, between whom there exist various literary connections. First, Day and Dekker collaborated on *The Bellman of Paris*, which was licensed by Henry Herbert in 1623. Secondly, the manuscript of Day's *The Parliament of Bees*, written between 1625 and 1634, contains twelve 'Characters', five of which also appear in *The Wonder of a Kingdom*, entered in the Stationers' Register in 1631 as 'by Tho: Decker'.[57] This was probably the same play as *Come See a Wonder*, which Henry Herbert licensed as Day's in 1623, and which was in all likelihood a collaboration between the two men. Furthermore, parts of *The Noble Spanish Soldier* by Dekker, which was entered to him in 1631 but may have been written c.1623, also appear in *The Parliament of Bees*. The relationship between these works has been much debated, but the most convincing explanation, put forward by Julia Gasper, is that Day was borrowing from the two plays by his friend Dekker when writing *The Parliament of Bees*.[58]

*

Guy of Warwick is based upon the medieval metrical romance of the same name and dramatizes the later events of the romance. Having won his love, Felice (Phillis in the play), Guy decides to leave his pregnant wife in order to undertake a pilgrimage to Christ's sepulchre in Jerusalem. He returns to England twenty-six years later, having performed remarkable deeds against the Saracens, and becomes a hermit, living at Guy's cliff in the forest of Arden. A subplot is provided by the comic interpolations of Sparrow, who accompanies Guy on his travels. The play ends with Guy's encounter with his son, Rainborne, but the hero dies before he can be reunited with his wife. Specific incidents in the play that are derived from the romance are Guy's injunction to Phillis regarding their child; King Athelstone's vision and encounter with Guy at Winchester gate; Guy's pre-battle prayer; Guy's encounter with Phillis; the angel's visit in Act V; and the story of Rainborne.[59] As has already been mentioned, the tower of Donather adventure derives from the romance *Huon of Bordeaux*. Crane also suggested that the Dun Cow is taken from the lost 1592 ballad *A plesante songe of the valiant actes of Guy of Warwicke* (which is the first appearance of the Dun

---

[57] Greg, *Bibliography*, i. 40.
[58] Julia Gasper, '*The Noble Spanish Soldier, The Wonder of a Kingdom*, and *The Parliament of Bees*: The Belated Solution to a Long-standing Dekker Problem', *Durham University Journal*, 79 (1987), 223–32.
[59] Crane, 'Vogue', 165, n. 75.

Cow in a literary context), and noted that the play's Jerusalem scenes were not supplied by the romance.⁶⁰ The play's comic subplot is also not derived from the romance of *Guy of Warwick*, being indebted, like the choric figure of Time, to theatrical rather than romance traditions. Comparable plays also related to romances are *Tom a Lincoln* and *Mucedorus*. *Tom a Lincoln* was never printed and survives in manuscript. It was probably composed between 1607 and 1619 and so is slightly earlier than the Day and Dekker *Guy* play. Time as Chorus and the clown Rusticano are additions to the play's source, Richard Johnson's *The Most Pleasant History of Tom a Lincolne* (1598–9 and 1607). Philip Sparrow (whose speeches in Act I are assigned to '*Clow*[n].') is similar to Rusticano in several ways. Both display an earthy sexuality that contrasts with the elevated sentiments of their masters, both are dialect speakers (Rusticano hails from Lincolnshire), both discourse perpetually upon their hunger and food, and their speech is peppered with Latin tags. Both clowns make reference to bagpudding (*Guy*, TLN 366; *Tom*, 470) and they both use the peculiar words 'Collefodiums' (*Guy*, 513) or 'Collosodiums' (*Tom*, 2071), which are unglossed in *OED* but, as G. R. Proudfoot has noted, the second probably signifies 'an ample buttock'.⁶¹ There are similarities in the comic business as well, particularly in the clowns' mistaking of persons. In *Guy*, Sparrow mistakes 'hermit' for 'emmot' (or 'emmet', a dialectal word for an ant) and so at first threatens to kill the old man, 'one of the fowleſt great Emmots | that ever I ſaw' (TLN 295–6), in emulation of Guy's battle with monstrous normality in the form of the Dun Cow. In *Tom*, Rusticano renders 'Prester John' as 'priest Si͞r Iohn' and so heads off into a detailed disquisition on the characteristics of his local parson. This section of ecclesiastical commentary celebrating the quotidian life of this country parson who tolerates maypoles and dancing on Sundays (*Tom*, TLN 1924–59), is itself reminiscent of the allusion to the Vestiarian controversy in *Guy* and the anti-puritan sentiments manifested there (*Guy*, 263–4). Given these similarities, M. C. Bradbrook's suggestion that *Tom a Lincoln* may be an Inns of Court burlesque of a Red Bull play, perhaps obtained from the Red Bull's manager and clown Thomas Greene, is potentially relevant to *Guy* as well.⁶² Viewed alongside the tentative link with Thomas Jordan of the Red Bull, and the fact that Dekker and Massinger's *The Virgin Martyr* was licensed for the Red Bull in 1620, the

---

⁶⁰ Crane, 'Vogue', 164.   ⁶¹ *Tom a Lincoln*, p. xxxi.
⁶² Bradbrook, 'A New Jacobean Play', 5, and her 'Shakespeare and the Multiple Theatres', in G. R. Hibbard (ed.), *The Elizabethan Theatre VI* (London and Basingstoke, 1978), p. 99, n. 15.

circumstantial evidence for the existence of a Red Bull *Guy* play (presumably that entered to Day and Dekker in 1620, and perhaps the text printed in 1661) seems strong.

The third clown play under discussion, *Mucedorus*, was printed in 1598, but is widely thought to date from about 1590. The clown part in this play is Mouse, who lacks the earthy sexuality of Sparrow and Rusticano, but shares to a certain extent their love of food: like Sparrow, he is partial to 'beef and brewis',[63] and there is a striking proximity of wording between his promise to Mucedorus of 'beef and brewis knockle-deep in fat' (IV. i. 69–70) and Sparrow's fantasy of 'a Platter of Bruis knockle deep in Fat' (*Guy*, TLN 367). Mouse is not a marked dialect speaker in the manner of Sparrow and Rusticano, but he does employ the occasional northernism, such as 'shipsticks' (II. iv. 67), meaning 'sheep's ticks'. The closest dramatic resemblance between *Guy* and *Mucedorus* comes in another comic confusing of 'hermit' and 'emmet'. Mucedorus adopts a hermit disguise, but Mouse falls prey to the same misprision as Sparrow, and makes the same deduction about the monstrous size of this 'emmet':

> *Mu.* I am an hermit.
> *Clo.* An emmet? I never saw such [a] big emmet in all my life before.
> (IV. i. 23–5)

Whilst there can be no doubt that the primary context for the printing of *Guy* in 1661 lies in the revival of pre-Restoration drama, certain features of the play suggest the possibility of a more local and specific, even political, appeal. As Nancy Klein Maguire and Derek Hughes have noted, serious drama of the early 1660s often addressed themes of usurpation, restoration, virtue, and recovery, the plays of the Earl of Orrery being a case in point. Against this background, the matter of *Guy* may well have seemed particularly congenial.[64] Guy's Christian piety and the play's emphasis on penitential practice may also explain its appeal, as might the story's connection with St George, a potent symbol in Stuart theatricals and self-articulations. For Charles I, as Annabel Patterson has argued, the figure of St George combined 'the ideals of warrior and saint, in an inarguably English embodiment' and emblematized 'a spiritualized and pacific chivalry'.[65] St George is

---

[63] *A Contextual Study and Modern-Spelling Edition of Mucedorus*, ed. Arvin H. Jupin, The Renaissance Imagination, 29 (New York and London, 1987), II. ii. 53–4.
[64] Nancy Klein Maguire, *Regicide and Restoration: English Tragicomedy, 1660–1671* (Cambridge, 1992) and Derek Hughes, *English Drama 1660–1700* (Oxford, 1996).
[65] Annabel Patterson, *Censorship and Interpretation: The Conditions of Writing and Reading in Early Modern England* (Madison, Wisconsin, 1984), p. 168.

invoked by Guy as he fights with Colbron, in a speech that exemplifies this style of Caroline chivalry and culminates with the lines 'St. *George* for *England*, lets begin the Fight, | Angels by me defend fair *Englands* right' (TLN 1008–9). As already noted, hints of royalist associations shadow the play and its possible contexts. Apart from the hypothetical connection with Thomas Jordan and the Red Bull, sketched above, there is a suggestive point of comparison with the royalist ballad-maker Matthew Parker, whose prose version of the *Guy* legend (probably in the form of a chapbook) was licensed in 1640 but is not extant. In this context, other items of note amongst Parker's literary output include his verse rendering of the romance *Valentine and Orson*, registered to Thomas Vere in 1658, and his *Most admirable Historie of that most Renowned Christian Worthy Arthur King of the Britaines* (licensed 1660); both works highlight the connection between royalist sensibilities and the reworking or revival of pre-Civil War romance and folklore material.[66] Furthermore, Helen Cooper's analysis of the play's anti-puritan stance on the Vestiarian controversy, whilst arguing in favour of an early date for the original *Guy* play, simultaneously provides another indication of why it would have appealed to newly restored Stuart tastes.

The play as printed in 1661 offers no conclusive answers as to its date of composition, authorship, or theatrical origins. Within the limitations of the available evidence, however, it would seem likely that there existed a play of *Guy* that can be dated c.1593–4, and which was subject to one or more stages of revision before being printed in 1661. The most likely intermediary stage is the Day and Dekker revision of 1620, which may have been a Red Bull play. It is also likely that this revision enhanced the latently tragic elements of the original, possibly playing down in consequence the affinities of the earlier play with historical drama, and favouring instead the themes of penitential piety and spiritual chivalry that can be observed in the 1661 edition. Despite the title-page's attribution of the play to 'B. J.', Jonson can be discounted as a possible author of the revision, whilst Day and Dekker are the most likely alternatives. Dekker's possible rewriting of the lost *Diocletian* as *The Virgin Martyr* at about the same time may offer an instructive parallel example of revision for the Red Bull undertaken on his release from prison. It also seems likely that this revised *Guy* play formed part of the transfer of copyrights from Wright to Gilbertson in 1655, especially given the presence of a closely related clown

---

[66] Hyder E. Rollins, 'Martin Parker, Ballad-Monger', *Modern Philology*, 16 (1919), 449–74, 458, 464, 470.

play, *Mucedorus*, within that collection of material; this could account for its re-emergence in 1661 despite the lack of an attested Restoration performance.

*

The present edition is a 1:1 photofacsimile of the Worcester College, Oxford, copy of the play. The play has been provided with Through Line Numbers (TLN), beginning with the title-page; the anomalous stage direction in smaller type on C4^v has not been separately numbered, but may be referred to as TLN 763+(1–5).

There are a few readings which, although decipherable in other copies of the quarto, may be unclear in the photofacsimile of the Worcester College copy:

Sig.	TLN	
A2^v	32–6	Time *now renues his fortunes to the world and layes them open to your Gentle Views ; think then with apprehenſive eyes you ſee this warlike Lord boldly attempt to fight, with that fell ſavage Bore of* Calledon
	41–2	*all for the love of* Phillis *he performs* ; *for* Phillis *love, old* Rohons *only Child,*
	54–66	*King.* Brave *Guy of Warwick*, honourable Earl, thus long in love and favour to thy ſelf King *Athelſtone* hath left fair *Wincheſter*, to frolick here with thee and thy fair Bride ; *Phillis* the comfort of old *Rohons* Age thus long to you we have been troubleſome, and uſed your Parkes and Paſtures as our own ; but now wee'l leave theſe parts of *Warwickſhire* and back again return to *Wincheſter*. *Guy.* Theſe Kingly favours that your grace hath ſhown, in honouring me a worthleſſe Subject thus, hath plum'd my thoughts with Eagle-flighted wings, and beares my mounting minde as high as Heaven,

A4ᵛ 184–6   nothing but death shall make me leave this Ring.
             Time calls me hence, fair *Phillis* now farewell,
             with thee let all Heavens joys for ever dwell. *Exeunt.*

     210–13   *Clow.* How comes the old Fox to know this trow; well I must
             set a good face on the matter or alls mar'd. Who I get her with
             Child? Father, why I take to witnesse the back-side of our
             Barn-door, I never kist her but twice in all my life.

THE
Tragical History,

Admirable Atchievments and various events
OF
GUY
EARL OF
WARWICK,
A TRAGEDY

Acted very Frequently with great Applause,
By his late MAJESTIES Servants.

Written by B. J.

Carpere vel noli nostra vel ede tua, Mart. Epig.

LONDON,
Printed for *Thomas Vere* and *William Gilbertson* without
Newgate, 1661.

THE
Tragical History
Admirable Atchievments and various events
OF
GUY
EARL OF
WARWICK
A TRAGEDY
Acted very Frequently with great Applause
by his late MAJESTIES Servants.

Written by B. J.

THE
Tragical History
OF
GUY
EARLE of *WARWICK*.

Actus Primus. Enter *Time*

IME *that is past, the Muses now recalls,*
forcing my fleeting presence to retire,
and pitch my feet upon the English shore,
I had almost drown'd in black oblivion,
an honour'd History of an English Knight,
as Famous once for deeds of Chivalry,
as any of the Worthies of the world:
Renowned Sir Guy of Warwick whose great Name,
makes England famous in all after times,
for nursing up so brave a Martiallist.

A 2   Time

The Tragicall History

Time now scannes his fortunes to the world,
and layes them open to your Gentle Views;
think then with apprehensive eyes you see
this warlike Lord, boldly attempt to fight,
with that fell savage Bore of Calledon,
that spoiles the fields and murders passengers,
him hath his sword subdu'd; and now again,
he combates with that huge and monstrous beast,
call'd the wild Cow of Dunsmore Heath;
all for the love of Phillis he performs
for Phillis love, old Rohons only Child,
what will not Guy of Warwick dare to do?
and having done those things that she enjoyn'd,
he reaps the harvest of her happy love,
and at the length enjoyes her for his wife.
To grace this bridal feast, imagine then,
King Athelstone hath left fair Winchester
and here in Warwick Castle keeps his Court.
VVhat follows now of Guy and his fair Deeds,
sit and behold, the story now proceeds.   *Exit Time.*

Enter King *Athelstone*, *Guy*, *Phillis*, *Rohon*, *Herod*, with others.

King. Brave *Guy* of *Warwick*, honourable Earle
thus long in love and favour to thy self
King *Athelstone* hath left fair *Winchester*,
to frolick here with thee and thy fair Bride;
Phillis the comfort of old *Rohons* Age
thus long to you we have been troublesome,
and used your Parkes and Pastures as our own;
but now wee'll leave those parts of *Warwickshire*
and back again return to *Winchester*.

Guy. These Kingly favours that your grace hath shown,
in honouring me a worthlesse Subject thus,
hath plum'd my thoughts with Eagle flighted wings,
and beares my mounting minde as high as Heaven

till

of Guy Earl of Warwick.

till I have done some deeds of Chivalry
Worthy the love of your Dread Majesty.

Guy. Which il'e perform with treble diligence,
and at your yearly Feast of Pentecost
will *Guy* of *Warwick* send a hundred Knights,
suddue'd and conquer'd by these Warlike Armes,
to do their Homage to King *Athelstone*,
lowly upon their knees at *Winchester*.

King. We thank thee *Guy*, but will not have it so,
live with thy love, thy sword hath won thee Fame,
and all the world doth speak of *Warwicks* Name.

Herod. The conquests that by thee hath been Atchiev'd,
makes men amaz'd, and warlike Knights affraid
to come in danger of thy Conquering Sword.

Lord. Thy manly deeds are Graven in each mans breast,
and thy large fame is spread from East to West.

Rohon. Live then in peace, my fair high-hearted Sonne,
since all men muse to think what thou hast done,
the *Calledonian* savage Bore is dead,
and by thy hand the wild Cow slaughtred,
that kept such Revels upon *Dunsmore* Heath;
and many adventures hast thou past beside
to make my Daughter *Phillis* thy fair Bride:
she now is thine, and all that I possesse,
is *Guy* of *Warwicks* so hee'l stay with us.

Phillis. Intends my honoured Lord to leave us then,
speak gentle love, my heart is full of fear;
O seek not danger, that is every where.

King. Content thee *Phillis* for he shall not go,
thy love intreats but we command him so,
And now Earl *Rohon*, reach the King thy hand;
Old man we thank thee and we take our leave;
Farewell Sir *Guy*, fair *Phillis* now adieu,
all earthly comfort still attend on you. *Exit King.*

Guy. Bright Angels still protect your Majesty,
Father conduct the King a little on his way, *Exit Rohon*
Sir *Herod* attend them, *Phillis* here, and I, *and Herod.*
must yet confer, wee'l follow presently.

Phillis.

The Tragicall History

   Phillis. What means my honour'd Lord to stay behind,
when every one attends his Soveraign;
why dost thou look so sad and stand so mute?
all looking downwards with thy care-craz'd head:
speak gentle love, if griefe thy mind oppresse,
Phillis will never leave thee comfortlesse.
   Guy. Ah *Phillis*!
   Phillis. Sweet: what hath *Phillis* done
that thy great heart should grieve to think upon?
   Guy. Nothing, O nothing, and I now to thee,
neither the fear of death, the losse of friends,
nor any thing this mortal life can yield,
doth trouble me or once molest my mind.
   Phill. What then disturbs thy high heroick Thoughts?
   Guy. That I must leave my *Phillis* whom I love;
O be not sad dear soul, but hear me speak;
for what I say must stand irrevocable.
Seven years to win thy love this Sword of mine,
hath beat down Monsters, and subdued strong Knights;
seven years to win thy love this breast of mine,
hath bin oppos'd even against the face of death:
But for my God who gave me power and strength
to doe these wonders in the sight of man,
hath *Guy* of *Warwicke* yet no service done,
the thought of which torments my inward soul;
and breaks my heart untill I have redeem'd
my great neglect of service to my God;
For which to him alone I have made a Vow,
never to lie by my fair *Phillis* side,
to eat, to drink, nor rest long in one place,
till I have seen my Saviours Sepulchre,
within the Walls of fair *Jerusalem*;
and with my Sword for my Redeemers sake,
beat back those misbelieving *Saracens*,
that seek the Ruine of that holy place,
making them leave deluding *Mahomet*,
and trust upon the blessed Name of *Christ*.
All this hath *Warwicke* sworn to undertake,

or

of Guy *Earl of* Warwick.

or loose his Life for his Redeemers sake.
  Phill. Sweet Lord!
  Guy. O do not bid me stay,
and ask me what thou wilt, I must away!
  Phill. See the rich burthen of my youthful womb,
the hopeful issue of thy happy love;
let that yet move thee, dear Lord do not go,
lest both of us do pine with grief and woe.
  Guy. Weep not sweet love; for tears will not avail;
but when the time comes thou art brought on bed,
and of thy child art safe delivered:
Give it to *Herod* if it be a a son,
with it deliver him this Ring of Gold;
tell him that I intreat him from my heart
that he will see my Infant well brought up;
bid him be kind to him, as I have been,
in all Adventures dangerous to him.
Now give me my Palmers Gown, my Hat and Staff,
these must I wear, fly hence all worldly pomp;
thus for my Saviour and Redeemer's sake
these blessed Weeds of Pilgrimage I take.
  Phill. My hearts so sad I know not what to say,
God grant thy Grave be not that Gown of gray;
My much misdoubting heart sayes I shall see,
my high loved Lord laid low in misery.
  Guy. Do not presage, dear love, but here me speak,
I charge thee on that love thou bearst to me,
never to reveal to Father, Friend, no nor the King himself,
what I intend nor whither I am gone;
until a month be past and I hence free;
for pursuit of my Friends will follow me.
Do this and *Phillis* love will brightly shine,
and *Guy* return with joy from *Palestine.*
  Phillis. I must, I will even do what you please,
your will shall be fulfilled yet ere you go;
this pledge of my true love I will bestow;
upon thy Hand I put my marriage Ring,
If ere I see the same and thou not by,

Phillis

The Tragicall History

Phillis will grieving weep, and weeping die.

Guy. I take thy pledge of love, and in exchange
I give this true loves kisse, and here I Vow,
nothing but death shall make me leave this Ring.
Time calls me hence, said *Phillis* now farewell,
with thee let all Heavens joys for ever dwell.

Enter Old Philip Sparrow, & his son the Clown.

Old. Dost thou hear me soon, zoon, zoon,

Clow. Never talk Father, never talk, for Youth will have his
swindge, if it be in a Halter; and I being a young Man and a
Scholar, will go travel to try the fruits of my Learning.

Old. But whither wilt thou go soon ha?

Clow. Faith Father, *Romo Romillus*, even to *Rome*, *Morter
moteribus*, with a Morter on my Head. But Father, Ile come
upon ye with a Verse, *Propria que maribones tribiunter masculæ
dogstones*.

Old. Whats that zoon ha?

Clow. That is, you must give me Forty pounds, and I must go
seek my fortune.

Old. Nay chil hold thee vorty of my teeth on that, the whorson
knave, and he'd tarry at home he might be Clark of our
Parish, so he might; he has his writing and reading Tongue, as
perfect as eating porredge, so he has; and sides all that, he spowts
Latin as vast as a Mill grinds fault; but che know the cause why
thoudst so vain be jogging.

Clow. Why Father?

Old. Nay chill tell thee with a witnesse, 'tis comported all about
our Parish that thou hast got our Neighbour *Sparling*
Daughter with Barne.

Clow. How comes the old Fox to know this trow; well I must
set a good face on the matter, or all's mar'd. Who I get her with
Child? Father, why I take to witnesse the back-side of our
Barn-door, I never kist her but twice in all my life.

Old. That thou shalt see, come hither *Parnell*. *Enter Parnell.*

Par

of Guy *Earl of* Warwick.

Par. O Mr. *Sparrow* I little thought you would have us'd me thus!

Clow. Why *Parnell* how have I us'd you? If there be ever a one in the Parish can use you better, let him take you and the Child too for me.

Par. But Mr. *Sparrow* you are not so good as your promise.

Clow. Nay *Parnell* never talk of that; for I have been better to you then my promise.

Old. How Knave, hast thou been better to her then thy promise, ha?

Clow. Why Father if you'l not bite off my Nose, Ile tell ye, I promised her to go home and eat a sowre Milk Posset; and if I have got her with child, 'tis more then my promise, and she's beholding to me for my labour.

Old. I sirrah, but you must marry her and make her amends.

Clow. How like an old fool you talk Father, why, she had more need make me amends; for I have made her look pritty and plump, and she has made me look like a shotten Herring. But Father take your blessing from me, for I must needs be walking.

Hony sops queen Maries pence,
Tears parts at going hence,
Ego volo Domine tu,
Sparrow will come with joy to you.

Old. Gods malediction go with thee good soon, Ah wees me, wees me.

Par. Farewel good Mr. *Sparrow.*   *Exeunt Old Man & Parnel.*

Clow. Nay do not cry good Father, do not weep sweet *Parnel,* but even farewel and be hang'd, thats twice God bo'ye; I made as though I had been sorry, but I could not weep and if I should ha been hang'd; but now will I go serve the bravest Man in all the world, his Name is Sir *Guy of Warwick*; they say he's going to *Jerusalem* and *Jerico*; but if he goes to the Divel I'le go with him, that's flat; and if *Parnel* be brought to bed before I come again, some honest Fellow do so much as pay for the Nursing of the Child, and Ile do as much for him another time.   *Exit.*

B   *Actus*

The Tragicall History

Actus Secundus.   Enter *Time*.

DEvotion and Divine Atchievments cause
Great Guy of Warwick to neglect all Lawes,
Of Nuptial League, he leaves his pregnant VVife,
Countrey and Kindred for a holy Life,
But in his progresse, makes himself a prize
To multitudes of matchlesse miseries;
By which it may be justly understood,
He is not truly great, that is not good:
In Holy Lands abroad his spirits roame
And not in Deanes and Chapters lands at home,
His sacred fury menaceth that Nation,
VVhich hath Indea under Sequestration:
He doth not strike at Surplices and Tippits,
(To bring an Oleo in of Sects in Sippits)
But deales his warlike and dead-doing blowes,
Against his Saviours and his Soveraigns foes;
That Coat of Armour fears no change of weather,
Where sanctity and souldier go together:
So doth our Champion march up to the fight,
Sit, silent, pray, Time will bring all to light.   *Exit.*

Enter *Guy* and *Sparrow.*

Guy. What Sirrah *Sparrow*?

Spar. Anon, anon Sir.

Guy. What are you turn'd Tapster since you came out of England?

Spar. Tapster quotha I shall never be so good a man while I live; for I had rather see a Tapster then a King: I like your long Journeys at Sea wel but for one thing.

Guy. What's that I pray?

Spar. O Master heres no Alehouses by the way, a man cannot

of Guy *Earl* of Warwick.

not get a Can of Beer for any Money; but Master why did you give that great Castle you got from the Gyant to that pueling harlotry in the silk Gown?

Guy. Why Sir she was a Lady of great birth.

Spar. A Ladle of great birch, why and she had been a ladle of holly; I would not have given't her I trow, you had bin better a given it me by half.

Guy. What wouldest thou have done with it?

Spar. I would have wrapt it in a Letter and sent it into *Warwickeshire* for a token: but Master, good sweet Master lend me your Sword.   *Enter an Hermit.*

Guy. What wilt thou do with it?

Spar. Here comes an Old man Ile kill him.

Guy. Ye cowardly Rogue wilt thou kill a Hermit?

Spar. An Emmot quotha, 'tis one of the fowlest great Emmots that ever I saw.

Guy. God blesse thee Father and send thee happinesse on Earth and Heaven when thou diest.

Spar. And the Gallowes when a dyes, what should he do with Heaven?

Her. O what art thou that speakest of God or Heaven, full forty Winters have I lived here, and never heard the Name of God till now, but in my prayers and my orisons.

Spar. A sawcy old Knave I perceive, he uses to eat Orrenges, Which very word makes me have an appetick as fierce as a Fidler at a Feast; it is a question of some difficulty, to resolve whether my Masters Spirit, or my Stomack be the greater; if he have the valour to knock down a Dun Cow, I have the Courage to Cut herup, and the Confidence to Carbonado her quarters.

Guy. Father into your private ears I dare,
power out my spirit, my designments are
for holy Actions, you may understand,
my pilgrimage is to the holy Land,
where my Redeemer's cause is trodden down,
where he wore Thorns, *Usurpers* wear a Crown,
I go to view the Monument and story
Of him that was no lesse then Lord of Glory.

Her. You answer punctually to what I ask,

B 2

but

The Tragicall History

but son you undertake a tedious task,
as intricate as dangerous, may I crave
the name of him whose valour is so brave?

   Guy. Although I now shrowded in these Pilgrims weeds,
(an holy habit fit for holy deeds)
I am an Earle, men call me *Guy* of *VVarwick*.

   Her. In all the space betwixt *Dover* and *Barwick*,
I have not known a man of clearer Fame,
(whose actions add new glory to his Name)
then he that owns that title, all that's good,
attend your Spirit and preserve your blood.

   Spar. And Father Emmot did you never hear of the Famous actions and valorous Atchievments of one Squire *Sparrow*?

   Guy. Away you Hedg-bird.

   Spar. Phillip is his Name,
A bird of *Venus*, and a Cock of the Game,
who once being in Love with pritty *Parnell*,
did crack her Nut, and thou maist pick the Kernell;
she is a Peacock every man doth vayle
his bonnet to her, when she shewes her tayle.

   Guy. Leave talking of your trundle Sirrah.

   Spar. VVhy so? my Mistris *Parnell* is as precious to me, as your Lady *Phillis* is to you, we have gotten them both with child; and all the difference is, that *Phillis* is your wedded VVife, and *Parnell* is my unmarried Mistris, and we must needs run up and down killing of Dun Cowes, Dragons, VVild-boars and Mastiff Dogs, when we have more work at home then we can well turn our hands to.

   Her. I like your high design, that for the truth,
can in the dayes of dalliance and youth,
prosecute piety, and attempt things
that Consecrate the Crowns of greatest Kings.

   Guy. Father your benediction will add wings   *Guy kneeleth.*
to all my undertakings.

   Her. May the springs
Of ever pregnant providence ne're be,
shut to your wants, but flow fertyle and free,
may you ne're feel necessities sharp rod,

                                                      the

of Guy *Earl of* Warwick.

the bleſſed Guardians of the higheſt God,
protect thy ſteps and keep thee far from ill;
ſo farewell Son my prayers attend thee ſtill.

Spar. Nay but do you here Old Man, pray let you and I have a two or three cold words together? Have you ever a Houſe here in theſe Woods?

Her. No Houſe but a poor Cottage, gentle friend.

Spar. Unch, How ſay ye? you would fain curry favour with me, but 'twill not ſerve your turn: Have ye ever an Ambry in your Cottage, where a Man may find a good Bag-pudding, a piece of Beef, or a Platter of Bruis knuckle deep in Fat; for I tell thee old fellow, I am ſharp ſet, I have not eat a good Meal this Fortnight.

Guy. Come hither Sirrah, can I no ſooner come into a ſtrangers Company, but you ſeek to diſgrace me!

Spar. Who I? why Maſter? you are mightily deceived in me, for I never uſe to ſay Grace before I ſee meat on the Table.

Guy. Sirrah, I ſpeak not of ſaying Grace but of Diſgrace, therefore Sirrah go and tell him you want no meat.

Spar. Shall I tell him ſo?

Guy. I Sir.

Spar. I ſhall tell him a monſtrous lye then.

Guy. You'l tell him ſo, quickly too if I intreat you.

Spar. Yes i'le tell him becauſe I dare do no otherwiſe; old man did I tell you I wanted meat?

Her. I marry did you.

Spar. Ye lye like an old Knave, yet if you have any Bread and Cheeſe about you, put a piece in my Cap.

Guy. Sir leave your prating, Father fare you well.

Her. More good attend thee then my tongue can tell. *Exit Hermit.*

Guy. This is the ſtately Tower of *Donather*,
where *Huon* of *Burdeaux* a couragious Knight
ſlew *Angolofar* in a ſingle Fight:
go *Sparrow*, ſeek find me an entrance in,
let me alone to cope with thoſe comes forth.

Spar. Why Maſter have you no more wit but to ſend me, did not you hear that there keeps a monſtrous Gyant in this Caſtle, that eateth a quarter of an Ox at a bit, his mouth's as wide as a barn

The Tragicall History

barn door, his eyes as broad as two pewter platters, and besides all that, they say, he hath Four and twenty Men to throw Mustard in his Mouth ; Now if I should come in the way, fall in the Mustard Pot, and be thrown into his mouth, you might go look for a man where you could get him.

Guy. I but you being a *Sparrow* methinks should flye from them.

Spar. O Master I must confesse I have been something loftily minded in my young daies, but *Parnell* and the rest of the pretty Wenches in our Parish have so pluckt my plumes, that I was never good mounter since ifaith.   *It Thunders and Lightens.*

Guy. Very well, then you'l not go?

Spar. Go, yes i'le go that's flat. O Master! the Divel, the Divel, the Divel.

Guy. Why? how now Sirrah, are you affraid?

Spar. No, I scorne to be affraid, but good Master for Gods sake grant me one request, upon my knees I ask it.

Guy. What's that Sir?

Spar. Sweet hony Master go your self.

Guy. I thank you Sir, but if you go not soon, my Sword shall bring you of a stomack to go.

Spar. O Master, never talk of that; for I have a stomack like a Horse, but no heart in the world to go to such a break-fast, but yet I'le go what somere comes ont, though I run into a bush presently; I am in Master, I am in.   *It Thunders & Lightens.*

Guy. It is no Gyant sure that keeps this place,
but some Inchanter or dam'd Sorcerer.
Hell-hound come forth, that I may cope with thee,
I fear not all thy charming Sorceries ;
send forth no shadows to afright my soul,
my Faith no Hell-born Fury can controul.

Enter the Inchanter.

Inchan. Let all my horrid Vapours cease their strength ;
Let the Air Freeze., the Earth be cold as Ice,
whereon this during Knight doth set his Feet.
For though Hells Force can no waies daunt his heart,
he soon shall know my Force can tame his Pride.

Guy.

Guy *Earl* of Warwick.

Guy. I cannot lift my Arms unto my Head,
my Feet stick fast into the solid earth,
and I shall never move my self from hence,
damned inchanter, hellish sorcerer,
whose black dam'd Art, hath wrought my lucklesse fall;
O that thou durst let loose this damned spell,
I soon would send thy fiend-like soul to Hell.

Inchan. By all the burning brooks of *Phlegiton*,
by *Styx* and *Acheron* I vow and swear
ne're shalt thou go alive out of this place.
Thus do I lay a charme upon thy head,
a hell bred slumber close thy sences up;
there groveling lye, and never more arise,   *Guy falls.*
a black inchanted charme close up thine eyes.   *Exit inchanter.*

Enter *Oberon* King of the *Fairies*.

Obe. But I will break thy charming Sorceries,
and he shall wake to be thy overthrow.
You harmlesse spirits of the flowry Meades,
Nymphes, Satyres, Fawnes, and all the Fairy train,
that waits on *Oberon* the Fairy King,
attend me quickly with your silver tunes;
and in a circled Ring, lets compasse round,
this sleeping Knight that lies upon the ground.

Enter the Fairies *with Musick, they Dance about him,* Oberon *strikes* Guy *with his Wand, he awakes and speakes.*

Guy. Where art thou *Guy?* what heavenly place is this?
what ravishing sound of Musick fills mine ear?
what blessed shadowes do appear to me,
that am a woful wretched sinful man?
O pardon me as I am faithful true,
I never yet meant hurt to none of you.

Obe. We know it well, arise fair Knight, stand up,   *Guy ariseth.*
                                                        thou

The Tragicall History

thou wert inchanted by a hellish fiend,
that doth inhabit in this hatefull Tower;
he casts thee in a deadly charming sleep,
and but by my means thou shouldest ne're have walkt,
I am the Fairy King that keeps these Groves,
for *Huon* of *Burdeaux* sake, thy Warlike friend,
the dear loved Minion of the Fairy King,
will I make *Guy* of *Warwicks* name be fear'd ;
for conquest of the Tower of *Donather*,
here take this charming Wand, I give it thee,
which is of such great vertue if it touch,
all the Inchantments in this spacious world,
they all shall be dissolv'd immediately.
For proof whereof make tryal against this Tower,
and in a moment it shall vanish hence.

Guy. Great Fairy King, how am I bound to thee,
that from these dangers hast delivered me,
I'le touch this Tower, if that dissolve these charmes,
Warwick is free from all inchanting harmes.

It Thunders, Lightens.
Enter Sparrow *running.*

Spar. Fire, Fire, Fire.

Guy. How now Sirrah, what's the news with you?

Spar. Whoop Master are you alive still? nay, then I care not ifaith, but I have been peper'd since I went from you.

Guy. How Sir I pray.

Spar. When you sent me to seek an entrance into the Castle, I thinking it was good sleeping in a whole skin, ran and hid my self in a bush, I had not lain there long but it began to Thunder and Lighten monstrously, and presently the Bush flew a Fire about my Eares; that with your favour I came away in a stinking complexity; but Master what fine little hop, O my Thumbs have you got here.

Guy. Sirrah take heed what you say for these are Fairies.

Spar. Fairies quotha, I care not what they be, I'le have about with them for a bloody Nose; I have a better stomack to fight with one of them, then with the Gyant a great deal; Unch ye whorson little pigpies, you i'le tickle ye ifaith.

The

of Guy Earl of Warwick.

The Fairies fall about him, pulls him down, pinches him, he cries out.

O Master help, help.

Guy. How now Sirrah, what's the newes with you?

Spar. I am kil'd master, I am kil'd.

Guy. Kil'd knave where art kil'd?

Spar. In the Buttock, in the Buttock.

Guy. Well Sir, rise, or i'le rise ye.

Spar. Rise quotha, yes, I'le rise, but I am sure I am dead; do you call these Fairies, a vengeance on them, they have tickled my Collefodiums ifaith; but master what is that same little gentlemans name?

Guy. Sir his name is King *Oberon.*

Spar. Little Gentleman is your name King *Colbron?*

Obe. No Sir, my name is King *Oberon.*

Spar. Why then good King Muttonbone learne your little Munkies to pair their Nayles with a pestilence; for my posteriors will feel the print of them this fortnight at the least.

Obe. Sir hold your peace, and *Guy* give me thy hand, the way i'le shew thee to the holy land, where I will add such glory to thy name that all the world shall speak of *Warwicks* fame. The black Inchanter he is gone to Hell, in endlesse torments ever for to dwell, Nymphs, Satyres, Fawnes, and all the rest march on, before stout *Guy*, and youthful *Oberon.*   *Exeunt.*

Actus Tertius.   Enter *Time.*

Thus swiftly runs the silent houres of *Time*,
whilst wordly men secured by their wealth,
think not on time nor on their soules fair health
but those whose well adorned lymbes are made,
of that pure mettal which shall never fade;
those that have learned of Angells how to sing,

C   *and*

The Tragicall History

and to the world all piety doth bring,
and fills the world with learning and with art,
to those doth Time her Golden gifts impart;
you fair beholders of this honoured story,
think now that Guy of Warwick he is gone,
leaving these Fairies and King Oberon,
and now to fair Jerusalem takes his way;
where hearing of the Wars the Pagans make
against that City and that holy Land,
he now prepares himself by force of Armes,
to save Judea from insuing harmes;
long stories are not told in little time,
much matter in small room we must combyne:
wee'l curtall nothing, yet make something short,
because we would shun tediousnesse of sport;
if it be long, say length is all the fault,
if it be lame, say old men needs must halt.

Enter *Sultan Shamurath*, Soldan of *Babylon*, with *Zorastes*.

Sult. Thus *Sultan Shamurath*, as Earthly God of Kings,
have marcht along with all their VVarlike Troopes.
Ten Thousand Gallies, ships and brigandines,
lye dancing on the Adratique Sea,
ready to be commanded when we please,
to bear this Captive King of fair *Jerusalem*,
to our Triumphant City *Babylon*;
but say *Zorastes*, how shall we employ
our VVarlike Forces 'gainst these Christians.
Most dread and mighty Emperour of the East,
whose puissant and warlike Force commands
even from the orient, to the sonnes decline;
suffer not thus these hated Christians
to inmure themselves in walls of stone and brasse,
whilst *Sultan Shamurath* with all his Lords
attends a day of battle with their swords.

Great

of Guy Earl of Warwick.

Great King of *Babell*, now be rul'd by me,
and let *Zorastes* counsel now prevail,
I'le raise up heaps of damned spirits from hell,
that shall make way unto my bold attempt.
Legions of Divels attend my dreadful Charmes,
ready to be commanded when I please;
then mighty *Soldan* make no more delay,
my art shall make the Conquerour this day.

Sultan. Thankes stout *Zorastes*, great Magician thanks,
but first lets summon them unto a parley
perhaps they'l yield their City to our hands,
knowing our force to be invincible,
and they not able to withstand our power.
Trumpet or Drum summon a parley there.

A parley sounded, Enter the King of Jerusalem upon the walls.

King. What craves *Thasirian* Emperour at our hands?

Sultan. Homage and fealty as thy Soveraigne Lord,
of all these spacious bounds of Christendome;
know petty King of fair Jerusalem
I am the mighty *Sultan Shamurath*
that rules the tripple City *Babylon*,
and all the Kingdomes of the Eastern world,
only this little part of *Asia*,
holds out against us and derides our faith
scorning our Lawes of holy *Mahomet*,
but by his blessed Alcaron I swear,
I'le ne're depart, nor draw my Army hence,
till in the Temples of *Jerusalem*,
both *Mahomet*, *Asteroth* and *Termagaunt*,
those holy Gods that Governs *Babylon*
be set for you stout Christians to adore,
which ye shall do, or all of you shall die,
and basely at our foot like Vassals lie.

King. Proud and Presumptuous Tyrant as thou art,
we fear no bug-bear threats of Tyranny,
nor all the multitudes thou canst command,
we guard and keep the blessed Sepulchre,

C 2 of

The Tragicall History

of our deare Saviour and Redeemer Christ,
within the walls of fair *Jerusalem*,
though on a suddain with your heathen Troops,
you have begirt us with a fearful siege:
yet know proud *Syrian* that fair *Zions* hill,
King *Solomon*'s Temple, and the marble Tomb,
which we adore with awfull reverence,
can raise a hundred thousand Christians
and proudly beat you back to *Babylon*.

  Sultan. Thou will not then surrender us thy Town?

  King. Not whilst one man survives to lift a sword,
attempt the worst you can, to save or kill,
we are prepar'd even against the worst of ill. *Exit King.*

  Sult. Why then at all, march forward warlike Lords,
wee'l parley now with Pole-axe, Bills and Swords,
darraigne our battles, and begin the Fight,
and *Mahound* still direct my course Aright.   *Exeunt Omnes.*

Enter Guy of Warwick *Solus.*

  Guy. Thus through the help of my dear Saviour Christ,
whose out-strecht arm hath still preserved me,
I am escap't from *Sultan Shamurath*,
and all his Hoast of cursed *Saracens*;
now I am come where I may fix mine eyes
safely upon King *David*'s City walls.
Is this *Judeas* pride, fair *Zions* hill?
Sanctum sanctorum and the house of Heaven,
the place where my dear Saviour lost his Life?
O how it grieves me to behold thy walls,
hem'd in with Dogs and cursed *Saracens*,
that seek to rob thee of thy beauty quite,
and turn thy joyful day to mourning night.
But heaven assisting me, I will prevent
their damned purposes, and make them repent,
their journey taken 'gainst *Judeas* good,

                              or

of Guy Earl of Warwick.

or in that fair adventure spend my blood.   *Enter Sparrow*

  Spar. Tarry, tarry, tarry, hold, hold, hold.   *crying.*

  Guy. Why? how now sirrah, what's the news with you?

  Spar. O Master are you there? I have done such an exploit as you never heard of in your life.

  Guy. What's that Sir?

  Spar. Nay, I am sure it passes your Capacity, but I'le tell you though, for it was a valiant piece of service, when I saw you got in amongst the *Pogons*, I thought some body had hired you to break heads by the dozen, for you never hit any of them, but they shak't their heels as though they had the Palsey; I seeing you so hard at work thought it not best to trouble ye, but after the old manner ran and hid my self in a bush.

  Guy. O Cowardly slave! was this your Valiant piece of service?

  Spar. O Master you doe not hear half yet, I lay so long till you were gone, and looking out of the bush, I could see all the *Pogons* laid fast asleep; then went I sneaking and stole away their Snapsacks with all their Victuals, I got up to the top of a Hill, and eat it up every bit, when I had done, I began to hollow; the *Pogans* missing their provant, came running after me, but I made one pair of Leggs worth two pair of Hands, and out-run them all ifaith.

  Guy. I thought what hot service you doe alwaies, but peace, here comes the King of fair *Jerusalem*.   *Enter the King*

  King. I am a wretched King, the more my wo, *of Jerusalem.*
Kings are sometimes distrest, and I am so,
but if thou be that warlike Conquerour,
that through the Pagan hoast hath cut thy way,
I do beseech thee even with woful tears,
to save *Judea Sion Palestine*
from base attempt of heathen servitude.

  Spar. If it be? O scurvy, if it be! why I'le tell you Goodman *King*, twas I and my master tickled 'um ifaith.

  Guy. True Sir, you and your Master and I, pray what did you?

  Spar. Why Master? when you had kil'd them, I came and cut off their Heads.

                                                          King.

The Tragicall History

King. Where wert thou borne? or whats thy Countries name,
brave Christian Knight, may I be bold to ask?

Guy. My Native Countrey is fair *England* cal'd,
my name Sir *Guy* of *Warwick*, hither come
of holy zeal to see my Saviours Tomb,
but seeing it hem'd round about with foes,
I cut a passage with my Warlike sword,
meaning to rescue it or lose my Life.

King. Heaven prosper thy attempt, lead on Fair Knight,
God and good Angels still protect our Right.

Guy. God and Saint *George* in *Warwicks* quarrel Fight.

Exit Omnes.

Alarum, Enter Sultan, Zorastes *from the Fight.*

Sultan. O speak *Zorastes*, what Divel or Man is that,
which in his Fury confounds such heaps of men?

Zorast. My Lord I cannot tell, but this I know,
neither *Turk* nor *Saracen* can withstand his blow,
our Souldiers fly like chaff before the Wind,
and none can stand against his Conquering sword.

Sultan. Canst thou not tell me what he is?
nor by thy Magick charmes confound the slave?

Zorast. I can do both as you shall streight behold;
Bellemoth, Ateroth Ascend.

Spirit. Quid me vis?

Zorast. I charge thee tell me truly who it is,
that in his rage confounds and spoiles our men.

Spirit. 'Tis *Guy* of *Warwick* that is hither come,
of holy zeal to see his Saviour Tomb.

Zorast. But never shall he see that Marble Grave,
go *Bellemoth*, and in a fierce flame,
hoyse him aloft into the vacant Air,
and throw him headlong into the Neighbouring Seas.

Spirit. Abeo.

Zorast. No, we fight my Lord, for victory is your's.

Sultan. Why? then *Zorastes* once more to the Fight,
and *Mahomet* direct my course Aright. *Exeunt Omnes.*
Alarum

Guy *Earl* of Warwick.

Alarum Excursions. Enter Sultan *and* Zorastes *flying,* Guy *and they Fight,* Zorastes *Escapeth,* Guy *taketh* Sultan *Prisoner.*

Then Enter the King of Jerusalem.

King. Command these brawling Drums to cease their noise,
whilst I salute our Warlike Conquerour,
renown'd Sir *Guy* of *Warwick*, whose great name,
extolls fair *England* with a glorious fame;
sit in our Throne victorious *Englishman*,
our Crown and Scepter shall be all as free,
to *Guy* of *Warwick* as it is to me.

Guy. Far be it from the thought of *Englishman*,
to usurp the seat of fair *Jerusalem*;
but for those favours you have grac't me with
here I resigne unto your princely hands,
Great *Sultan Shamurath*, King of *Babylon*.

King. Victorious Knight, both in thy words and deeds,
this proud presumptuous King of *Babylon*
which thou surrendrest here as prisoner,
I freely do deliver back to thee,
to ransome or dispose as thou thinkst best.

Sultan. Let me be ransom'd mighty Christian Knight,
and I will back surrender to thy hands
all those Townes and Castles I have won,
Joppa, *Samaria* and Rich *Nazareth*,
with fifty Thousand bars of silver plate,
to ransome home great *Sultan Shamurath*.

Guy. I scorn thy league and love, proud heathen King,
I'le make thee now my Vassals underling.

Sultan. Scornst thou to love the Monarch of the world?

Guy. The Monarch of black Hell, should I not scorn,
the love of *Belzebub Leviathan*,   *Sultan stamps.*
Nay Sir I'le make you tear your Mahomet,
and stamp and stare.
                      Enter Sparrow with a
                      Pagan in a Halter.
                      Spar.

The Tragicall History

Spar. I and swear too ifaith afore I have done with him; O Master you think I can do nothing, I have catcht a *Pogon.*

Guy. How sir I pray?

Spar. Why Master after the valliantest manner that could be; for I found him asleep, and having a Halter in my pocket, put it about his Neck instead of a falling band.

Guy. But what will you do with him now?

Spar. Marry Master, first and come fordermost, I'le hang him two houres by the Clock, then i'le cut off his head becaufe he shall not call me knave for my labour; and when I have done so, I'le let him go his way, nay ye whorson *Pogon* I'le tickle ye that's flat; O Master the *Pogon* has given me two slips for a Tester, but I'le after him, if I catch him again, I'le give him a Cawd cast in's Chaps, that's two turns and a wry mouth, and then he may drink to his friends all the day after.

The Pogan takes the Halter from his own Neck, and put's it about Sparrows neck, and runs away.

Exit Sparrow.

Guy. Since that your Majesty hath back delivered,
this *Sultan Shamurath* into my hands,
know the ransome I will set on him,
shall please our God and all good Christians.
O blessed Emperour think upon the Crosse,
which is the true badg of our sweet Saviour Christ
by whose great help we have got Victory.
Then to enlarge the Fame of Christendome,
and our great makers ever glorious name,
Thou *Sultan Shamurath* with all thy Hoast,
shall leave your faith and become Christians;
do this, from any ransome thou art free,
and all thy people set at liberty.

Sult. We yield consent victorious Conqueror,
the God you serve is great Omnipotent,
ruling the day of battle as he please,
making one hundred kill ten thousand men,
such were the odds of our Battallions;
therefore for *Guy* of *Warwicks* sake,
wee'l trust in Christ, and *Mahound* clean forsake.

King.

of Guy Earl of Warwick.

King. Then fit we honour'd to the Marble Tomb,
where you shall have received your Christendome,
you and your Lords shall take a Solemne Oath,
that all your Empery shall do the like;
come on brave *Guy*, for by thy hand is done,
this Everlasting fame to Christendome.

Exeunt King and Sultan.

Guy. Go on great Kings, I'le follow presently,
and now since all those wars are at an end,
and that my heavenly Maker hath vouchsaft
to give me victory against his foes,
in lowly Pilgrimage I vow to come,
and visit my dear Saviours blessed Tomb;
there for an everlasting memory,
I'le offer up my sword and furniture,
and here I make a vow in sight of Heaven,
that henceforth i'le never bear Armes again,
but spend the residue of my sinful Life,
in zealous Prayers and repentant Tears,
for all the follies of my wretchlesse youth.
Now glorious God with thy Auspicious eye,
smile on this happy work that's thus began,
to enlarge the fame of blessed Christendome.   *Exit.*

Actus Quartus. Enter *Time.*

THus *Time* that in his ceaslesse motion,
controuls the hearts of *Kings* and *Emperours*,
hath now converted Sultan Shamurath
to tread the path of perfect Christendome;
and now with Bishops, Priests *and* Patriarks,
they are returned back to Babylon,
to Christen all that Heathen Nation;
think this is done, and now again suppose,
that Guy of Warwick after he had seen

D   bis

The Tragicall History

his *Saviours Tomb, and there had offered up*
as Monuments of lasting Memory ;
his sword, his shield, and Warlike Furniture,
he there vow'd never to bear Armes again,
and now towards England *is returning back.*
Imagine that Sir Raynborn *his fair son,*
is grown a man, and hearing of the deeds
of his great Father, leaveth all his Friends
to seek him out in Forrain Nations.
Think this is done, and now again suppose
that Guy of Warwick *now is waxen old,*
and at the length of many a weary step,
he comes to England, *where perforce alas*
he must oppose, his weak decayed limbs
against the vigor of a Gyants strength ;
for now the Danes in absence of this Lord,
have set their feet so far on Englands *ground ;*
that they had almost conquered all the Land,
and to a forced Parley drives the King ;
how they conclude, and by what means agree,
Time shall make known to you immediately. **Exit Time.**

Enter Swanus *King of* Denmark, *with him* Colbron.
Then Athelstone *King of* England, *with him* Herod.

Athelstone. Swanus *of* Denmark, since to this Enter-view,
by thee appointed, we here both are met,
Speake what canst thou demand from *Englands* Crown?

Swanus. Thy Crown and Kingdome is by conquest won,
yet if thou canst provide a Champion,
that dares encounter mighty *Colbron* here ;
if he that Fights for thee, do win the day,
all Title to thy Crown wee'l lay away ;
but if that *Colbron* gets the day in field,
the English power to the *Danes* shall yield ;
and then thy homage and thy Princely Crown,
will *Swanus* bear to *Denmark* as his own.

Athelst. I force, perforce must yield to thy demand,

but

of Guy Earl of Warwick.

But had I *Guy* of *Warwick* thou shouldst know,
thy Gyants force he soon would overthrow.
   Colbron. I tell thee King, no weak-bred arm of thine,
can shed one drop of mighty *Colbrons* blood,
whilst I have power, or any strength to stand,
or grasp this Truncheon in my Warlike hand;
for in my Fury I will take my Foe,
and fling him higher then the Moons bright sphear,
then bandying back the Foot-ball of my rage,
cast him down headlong to the Neighbouring Seas.
   King. No more, no more, to morrow is the day.
   Swanus. When Might or Right shall bear the Crown away.
                                    Exeunt.

Enter Guy *being Old.*

   Guy. Thus one and Twenty Winters have I been,
a very stranger to my home-bred soyle,
and never set my Feet on English ground;
in Foraign Countries have I eat my bread,
and now bring Winter on my Snow white-head;
which of my Friends that meets me by the way,
will once imagine that I am Sir *Guy*,
that vanquisht Knights, and made stout Monsters die.
O, no not one, will once remember me,
beauty and youth so little lasting be.
What place is this, wherein I am Arrived?
I know it well, 'tis call'd fair *Winchester*,
whereas King *Athelstone* doth keep his Court,
the nights far spent, and my age withered limbs,
are weak, and weary, with long travelling;
here will I sit and rest my self a while,   *He sleepeth.*
and with sweet sleep my wanward thoughts beguile.
               Enter Athelstone with Guy, disguis'd.
   Lord. What means your Majesty, thus carelesly
to walk abroad without your wonted Guard?
   Athelst. I'le have no Guard, unlesse thy self with me,
for know this Night as I lay in my bed,
               D 2   a bles-

The Tragicall History

a blessed Angel bright and Christaline
in golden slumber did appear to me,
bidding me walk out of my Castle Gate,
and the first man that I should meet withal,
choose him my Champion to defend my right,
which makes me rise thus early, for to see *Guy starts from*
this heaven bred Champion sent to let us free. *his sleep.*

  Guy. Give me my Sword, mine Armour, and my shield,
that I may Coap with *Hybean Hercules* ;
the horrid villain in a Centaures shape
hath ravisht *Layda* on her wedding day ;
therefore I hand to hand will Coap with him
were he the Master Monster of the world :
alas where am I poor distressed Man ?
my troubled mind utters I know not what,
thou Fight with Monsters, Fight thou with thy grave,
and for thy sins humble forgivenesse crave:
But out alas, I fear I am o're-heard, *He espies the King walking.*
I will enquire of these the ready way
that leads directly to your City fair ;
good morrow, and God blesse you Gentleman.

  Athelst. Good morrow Father.

  Guy. May I be bold to crave which is the way,
that leads directly unto *Winchester ?*

  Athelst. This path good Father leads to *Winchester.*
O heaven what should I think my dream pretend,
that will'd me choose the first man I should meet;
but this good Aged man is far unfit,
yet will I ask his Counsel in this cause
that may avail me far more then his strength,
good Father may a stranger be so bold
to have some private conference with thy self?

  Guy. Speak on good Sir and what so e're it be,
My truth I give to keep it secretly.

  Athelst. Then know good Father that I am a King,
my Courts beset with many Enemies,
and this last night as I lay in my bed
a Heavenly Vision did appear to me,
bidding me rise up streight and walk abroad,
and the first man that I should meet withal,

choose

of Guy Earl of Warwick.

choose him my Champion to defend my right;
thou Aged Father art the first I meet,
but he that doth maintain this Fight,
is a most monstrous Gyant huge and strong,
and thou art feeble, weak and impotent,
yet thy Counsel Father, what I were best to do?

Guy. Do as Heaven wills, ye do my Gracious Lord,
if by the all fore-seeing power thereof,
I am appointed for to do this deed;
though I be old, yet you shall well perceive,
I'le not give back nor yield one foot of ground;
what though he be a Gyant that maintaines
this deadly combate? ere I'le turn my face,
I'le leave my body breathlesse in this place.

Athelst. O how glad's my very Soul to see
a youthful mind in Aged Livery!
come Reverend Father, for thou now shalt be,
a Kings companion that will honour thee.

Guy. Go on great King, an old man once will try,
the Vigor of a churlish Gyants strength;
though he be huge and strong with whom I Fight,
my God is just and still maintaines the right. *Exeunt.*

Enter Swanus and Colbron.

Swanus. Now *Colbron* rowse thy Gyants setled limbs,
for all our blessed hopes on thee we lay,
thinking to bear the English Crown away.

Colbr. I tell thee King thou troublest me with doubts,
for halfe their Kingdome is already won
by *Colbron* and the *Danish* Conquerours,
upon the rest I will sharp vengeance take.
Where are these faint-hearts? O that they were come,
that I might finish up a day of Doom!

Swanus. I hear them coming, therefore lets prepare,
to bid them welcome to a bloody feast,   *Enter Athelstone with*
for I perceive they all are resolute.   *Guy and others.*

Athelstone. Swanus of *Denmark*, see wee keep our word,
and come to try our right by dint of Sword.

Swa. Bring forth thy Champion.

Athelst. Here he stands prepar'd.

Swanus. O, who? he alas poor silly man,
give him a pair of Beads to pray upon.

Athelstone. Scorn him not *Swanus*, for this old mans hand,
against thy mighty Gyants force shall stand.   *Colbron.*

The Tragicall History

Colbron. Must *Colbron* Fight with such a withered Ghost,
a very shrimp, a worm, a gnat, a fly,
I scorn him and will spurn him at my feet.

Guy. Leave of thy braves, blaspheming heathen dog,
for God whose quarrel I do take in hand
will add fresh strength to these my withered limbs,
these aged sinews that are weak and old,
he can renew with monster conquering strength;
therefore to shew, I do not fear thy threats,
sound an Alarum lets begin the Fight,
for with my Palmers staffe i'le coap with thee.

Athelst. Thou shalt not hazard so thy honoured age,
begirt thy self with these wars Ornaments.

Guy. What shall I do? unhappy wretched man,
for when I left the wars of *Palestine*,
I made a vow even in the sight of Heaven
never to Fight with Sword or Shield again;
but I must break that vow, or leave this Land,
my Native Country to the violent hand;
of damned Usurpers, which shall never be,
I'le break my Oath, and sweet Heaven pardon me.
Here do I take this Sword into my hand,
and buckle fast this shield unto my Arme,
although I know it is no armed hand
that can prevail, but Heaven where truth doth stand;
and now thou great Arch-guyder of the world,
that saved *Daniell* in the Lyons Den,
look down on me, with thy all-pitious Eyes,
and by my Hand vanquish thy Enemies,
that all may say in Glory to thy name,
that little *David* hath *Goliath* slain;
St. *George* for *England*, lets begin the Fight,
Angels by me defend fair *Englands* right.

Colbron. In *Mahounds* name I do thee here defie,
for I will crush thy bones immediately.

     They Fight, Guy killeth Colbron.

Athelst. St. *George*, St. *George*, *England* hath prevail'd,
              and

Guy *Earl* of Warwick.

and *Denmark* and his Champion now are quaild.
   Swa. Mahound Confound that old mans hellish Armie,
that hath wrought *Englands* good, and *Denmarks* harm;
now force perforce, to *Denmark* we must go,
ne're had the *Danes* so great an overthrow.   *Exit Swanus.*
   Athelst. Since by thy means most Reverend Aged Man,
I and my Country are delivered,
from the usurping *Danish* Tyrants power,
I conjure thee by that holy vow
which thou didst make in taking on this weed,
of thy religious holy pilgrimage;
tell me thy name, and what thy Countries call'd,
which was so happy as to Foster thee.
   Guy. Upon Condition that your Majesty,
will vow to keep close what I shall reveal,
I will resolve your princely mind at full.
   Athelst. Speak freely then, for what so e're it be,
upon my word I'le keep it secretly.
   Guy. I take your princely word then know great King,
I am your Subject and in *England* born,
and many favours have receiv'd of you,
past the deserts of my unworthinesse;
for which it glads my soul that e're I dye,
I have done some service for your Majesty.
When I was young, men knew me by my looks,
but now the hand of age hath chang'd me so,
that not one man doth *Guy* of *Warwick* know.
   Athelst. So said my soul, when I first saw thy face,
welcome, O welcome, to thy Native soile,
which thou hast freed from ruine and from spoil;
and ten times welcome art thou unto me,
thy absence long hath wrought my misery,
But tell me, hast thou seen fair *Phillis* yet?
   Guy. My Lord I have not, nor I do not know,
whether my beloved *Phillis* lives or no.
   Athelst. I can assure thee that thy *Phillis* lives,
but her old Father *Rohon* he is dead;
Sir *Rainborn* thy couragious hearted Son,   *Guy weeps.*

hath

The Tragicall History

hath been these two years for to seek thee out,
why weepst thou *Guy*?

Guy. I weep for joy to hear this happy news,
hath *Guy* of *Warwick* then a Kingly Son?
and is fair *Phillis* still in perfect health?

Athelst. She is good *Guy*, and i'le send speedy post,
to *Warwick* Castle for to fetch her hither.

Guy. O I beseech your grace to give me leave,
an end of this my Pilgrimage to make;
for when I took my way *Palestine*,
I made a vow for seven and twenty years
to keep my self unknown from all my Friends;
full one and twenty are expired and gone,
six more being past, I from my vow am free,
and then to all my friends disclos'd i'le be.

Athelst. I must consent, since thou will have it so,
but at the six years end i'le come to thee,
and with me I will bring so rich a Train,
as shall in state, bring *Warwick* home again;
till then I leave thee to thy sweet content,
willing my life for thy good be spent.   *Exit King.*

Guy. Farewel my Liege, Farewel my Soveraigne,
and now poor *Guy*, since thou art left alone,
think on thy Makers mighty love to thee,
who in thy youth did make thee fear'd of all,
and by thine age hath wrought a monstrous fall;
he hath preserv'd thy true and faithful Wife,
whom thou didst love more dearer then thy Life;
to her i'le go as fast as I can hye,
but shee'l not think that *VVarwick* is so nigh:
ah *Phillis*, now thy Lord is waxen old,
who when thou sawest him last was stout and bold;
yet as I am, I'le sek my *Phillis* Face,
if he that made me gives me Life and space,
I'le tell her tydings of mine own estate,
and fetch my food at my own Castle Gate;
And for six years which I alone must lead.
Phillis must feed her unknown Lord with bread.   *Exit.*

Actus

of Guy Earl of Warwick.

Actus Quintus. Enter Time.

THus Guy to Warwick *Castle now is gone*,
where hearing of the Almes fair Phillis *gives*
to Palmers, that do daily passe that way;
he thither goes, and at her hand receives
his daily food; and being unknown,
he tells her tidings of his own estate;
and in a forrest not far from the place,
a mile distant called Arden *wood,*
with his own hands he builds himself a Cave.
What followes now of Rainborn *his fair Son,*
Sir Herodes *meeting, and of their return,*
and what to Guy *of Warwick doth befall,*
sit pleas'd a while and Time shall shew you all.   Exit Time.

Enter Guy Solus.

Guy. Now am I come in sight of my fair Home,
thats cal'd *Guye's* Crosse, for that I did erect,
before I went to fair *Jerusalem*;
here was I wont to sit and view my Land,
and eke my Castle that on Tiptoes stand,
to overpeer this part of *Warwickshire*.
                                  Enter two Palmers.

1 *Palmer.* Come hither, lets a little mend our pace,
for we are near to *Warwick* Castle now;
where I have heard of late fair *Phillis* dwells,
who gives Almes to all that passe that way.

2 *Pal.* Good brother lets go thither presently;
but stay, methinks here sits an Aged man,
lets ask him if hee'l go along with us?

1 *Pal.* With all my heart;
all happinesse attend you Aged Father.

Guy. The like I wish to you good gentle Friends.

1 *Pal.* May we intreat you go along with us,

E

The Tragicall History

to *Warwick* Castle, where fair *Phillis* dwells,
who giveth Almes to all such as we are.
   Guy. With all my heart, I'le go along with you.
                Enter Phillis, *and a Servant with Bread and Wine.*
1 *Pal.* See where she comes out of her Castle Gate.
                     Both Palmers *kneel and pray.*
Heaven blesse fair *Phillis* for this deed,
and send Sir *Guy* of *Warwick* home with speed.
   Phillis. Amen, Amen, come give them a reward,
there's Bread and Wine, eat and refresh your selves;
and there's some Money to relieve your wants,
and pray for *Guy* of *Warwick,* and his Friends.
But wherefore stands this Aged man so sad?
What art thou Father?
   Guy. A poor distressed Pilgrime gentle Lady.
   Phill. More welcome art thou unto *Warwicks* Wife.
for in a Pilgrims weed my Lord is gone,
even to the furthest part of Christendome.
But tell me Father, hast thou travel'd far?
   Guy. Lady I have, and seen my Saviours blessed Sepulchre.
   Phillis. In all thy travels didst thou never hear
of *Guy* of *Warwick,* and his Warlike Deeds?
   Guy. I have both heard, and been with him,
even at the siege of fair *Jerusalem*;
where he perform'd such deeds of Chivalry,
that by his means the City was preserv'd,
and *Sultan Shamurath* with all his Hoast,
was overcome and holy vanquished.
   Phillis. Let me embrace thee in my tender Armes,
and kisse thy Aged Cheek, for until now,
of my dear Lord, I never heard so much;
reach me a stool, I prethee Father sit.
   Guy. Here on the ground I'le sit, tis earth and dust,
from it I had my Birth, to it I must.
   Phillis. Give me some Bread? I prethee Father Eat.
   Guy. Give me Brown Bread, for thats a Pilgrimes Meat.
   Phillis. Reach me some Wine, good Father tast of this.
   Guy. Give me cold Water that my comfort is,
                                  I tell

of Guy *Earl of* Warwick.

I tell ye Lady your great Lord and I,
have thought our selves as happy as a King,
to drink the water of a Christal spring.

Phillis. O do not break my sorrow beaten heart,
with sharp remembrance of his miseries,
that is more dear to me then all the world;
but gentle Father for this happy newes,
which thou hast told me of my beloved Lord;
if in my Castle thou wilt stay with me,
for *VVarwicks* sake I will make much of thee.

Guy. I thank you Lady, but I cannot stay,
my hast in Pilgrimage calls me away;
therefore in duty here I take my leave.

Phillis. O stay a while, and do not go so soon,
for I am loth to leave thy company;
this poor reward of *Phillis* shalt thou take,
which I do give thee for my *Warwicks* sake;
so fare thee well, whatsoe're the cause should be,
my heart is full of grief to part with thee.

Exit Phillis and her Servant.

Guy. And mine of sorrow and deep misery.

1 *Pal.* Come Father, will you along with us?

Guy. Go on good friends, I follow presently,   *Ex. Palmers.*
as fast as weakned age will give me leave.
And now poor *Guy* fall prostrate on thy knees,
and thank the God that gave thee such a Wife;
Phillis when thou art dead and laid in grave,
few such true Women will fair *England* have.
Now will I hye me unto *Arden* wood,
there in a Rock of stone I'le build a Cave;
and of my *Phillis* fair, whom I love best,
i'le fetch my daily Food, and thus in rest
till full six years be brought unto an end,
unknown to any, I my life will spend.   *Exit Guy.*

E 2   Enter

The Tragicall History

Enter Rainborne *Solus.*

Rain. Now that the poasting Charet of the Sonne,
hath tired *Phœbus* and his wanton steeds,
the duskey Clouds hath closed up the day,
and *Hesperus* is left to guide the world;
Here *Rainborne* rest thy self within these woods,
and give thy weary limbs some time of stay,
until that *Phœbus* chase the night away;
then will I buckle on my Armes again,
and never cease pursuit till I have found
my Warlike Father, the renown'd Sir *Guy*, *He sits down.*
which I will doe, or in this journy dye.

Enter Sparrow. A Pilgrimage quotha, marry here's a Pilgrimage indeed, why? I have lost my Master, and have been this fortnight in a Wood, where I have eat nothing but Hips and Hawes, that ye may make Fiddle strings of my Guts they are so thin: but I am serv'd well enough; for when I was at home with my old Father, where I had my belly full of Beef and Bag-pudding, but I must be Travelling with a Pestilence.

He espies Rainborne.

But stay, who have we here? some Traveller I hold my Life on't, I care not greatly if I knock out his Brains, and then take away all his Money, yet sure he has not much, he has such fine Cloaths on; for commonly now adaies our Gallants in their Silkes and Velvets have the Divel dancing in their great Hose; for there's never a crosse to hinder him, therefore I'le wake him sure, Whoop whow, *&c.*

He Hollowes in his Ear.

Rainborne. How now Sirrah, what are you?

Sparrow. A Curstian, what art thou?

Rainborne. Art thou a Christian? prethee where wer't born?

Sparrow. Ifaith Sir I was born in *England* at *Stratford* upon *Aven* in *Warwickshire.*

Rainborne. Wer't born in *England*? what's thy name?

Spar.

of Guy Earl of Warwick.

Sparrow. Nay I have a fine finical name, I can tell ye, for my name is *Sparrow*; yet I am not no house *Sparrow*, nor no hedge *Sparrow*, nor no peaking *Sparrow*, nor no sneaking *Sparrow*, but I am a high mounting lofty minded *Sparrow*, and that *Parnell* knows well enough, and a good many more of the pretty Wenches of our Parish ifaith.

Rainborne. Very well Sir, what make you here in these Countries?

Sparrow. Marry I have lost a stray Master, can you tell me any tidings of him?

Rainborne. What was thy Masters name?

Sparrow. My Masters Name, why you would not hear it would ye?

Rainborne. Yes sir that I would.

Sparrow. Well he has a tickling name I can tell ye.

Rain. Howsoever let me hear it.

Spar. Yes you shall hear it, he is cal'd the most Couragious, Bravagious, Contagious; but do you hear young Gentleman, have ye ever another suit of apparel ne're hand.

Rain. VVhy Sir?

Spar. VVhy truly all will not be well with ye if you hear my Masters name; therefore I would wish you take heed what ye doe, for you'l perfume that, so that ye will have need of another.

Rain. Sirrah leave your prating, and let me hear it.

Spar. Nay ye shall hear it, he is called the most Renowned, Profounded, Compounded; but heark ye, have ye ever a clean shirt about ye?

Rain. VVhy Sir?

Spar. VVhy? I know if you hear my Masters name you'l blow your Nose backward, and then your Landresse will call you Sloven.

Rain. Why ye base Pesant, shall I not hear his Name?

Spar. O Lord Sir, ye are deceived! I am no Phesant, though I be a *Sparrow*, yet you shall hear my Masters name, he is called Sir *Guy* of *Warwick*.

Rain. Sir *Guy* of *Warwick*, my Renowned Father.

Spar. Thy Father, thy Halter, indeed when I came out of
England

The Tragicall History

England I left a Wench pretty and plump, thou may'st be my Son, if thou beest, kneel down and ask me blessing, and i'le give thee two pence.

Rain. Away you base slave.

Spar. Why dost thou think scorn to ask me blessing?

Rain. I Sir that I do.

Spar. Then I think scorn to give thee my two pence.

Rain Sir leave this talk and tell me certainly, where brave Sir *Guy* at this time doth remain, and with rich gifts I will requite thy pains.

Spar. VVill ye so, why the last time I saw him he and I were going towards *England*, and in the midst of a great wood I lost him, but I had better have been hang'd or some worse mischance come to me, for I am like never to get home as long as I live.

Rain. Nay fear not that, for if thou't stay with me, for VVarwicks sake I will make much of thee.

Spar. But are you Sir *Guy* of VVarwicks Son?

Rain. Upon my Knightly word I am.

Spar. Faith I doubt you are some lying Hangman; for indeed we Travellers may lye by Authority; but I'le tell ye what I'le doe, stay you here till I go into *England*, and ask your Mother, if she sayes so, I'le come again and then I'le dwell with you

Rain. Nay stay Sir, for it is above a Thousand mile into *England*.

Spar. A Thousand mile, nay sure i'le take your word before i'le go so far to try the matter, but if I should be content to dwell with you, what dyet will you allow me?

Rain. Why Sirrah? to your Dinner you shall have a Pomgarnate.

Spar. A pound of Garlike, why I never eat Garlike in all my Life;

Rain. I say a Pomegarnate, which is almost like an Apple.

Spar. Apples to my Dinner, and what to my Supper? quickly, quickly.

Rainborne. Why to your Supper you shall have a Couple of Olives.

Spar.

of Guy *Earl of* Warwick.

Spar. Nay that's not much amisse, for that is two leggs of Beef stuft with Parsley.

Rain. You are deceived Sirrah, for an Olive is no bigger then a Plum.

Spar. How Apples to my Dinner, and Plums to my Supper, O my belly, my belly, my belly; why Master you have kil'd me already, but i'le tell ye how ye must use me; at Eight of Clock you must call me up; but ye must not make too much hast, for I must have half an hours scratching before I can put on my Shirt; then betwixt nine and ten I must be at breakfast, and from eleven to one at Dinner, then I must go to sleep till three, then I must have my Afternoons Nunching, then at five of the Clock my Supper; and then what work you will all the day after, but you must not feed me with Apples and Plums, for I must have my fill five times a day of Beef, Brewis, Bag-Puddings and Pies. Oh how my Teeth waters to think on them, besides odd bits in a Corner; and if you'l deal thus with me, I'le dwell with you, and doe all this that I have promised you.

Rain. That's eat your Victuals and sleep.

Spar. Why aye and something else too, though it be no great manners to speak on't.

Rain. But art thou sure my Father is gone for *England*?

Spar. Am I sure? why I tell ye, he is in *England* long ago.

Rain. Why then in hast i'le post to *England* now.
but I'le not tarry in it, nor else where,
unlesse I find my Warlike Father there;
Come *Sparrow* follow me.

Spar. Do you hear young Master, though you be my Master, yet I am your Elder, and therefore your better, and alwaies while ye live, learn to let your betters go afore ye. *Exeunt.*

Enter Guy *Solus.*

Guy. Thus have I almost brought unto an end,
the tedious time of my long Pilgrimage,
for of my seven and twenty years remains

only

The Tragicall History

only seven days to be accomplished.
The longest Summers day comes to an end;
The dials point though none perceive it stur,
in length of time creeps round about the same;
even so this long thought time is almost spent,
onely seven dayes to come, and I am free,
and then to all my Friends disclos'd i'le be.
        Enter an Angell.
 Angell. Thou blessed Champion of the highest Heaven,
be firme in faith, and here my message out,
for my great Master sends thee word by me,
that seven dayes being past thou sure shalt dye;
tears change not fate, poor pilgrime now farewel
go meet more joyes then Angels Tongues can tell.
        Exit Angell.
 Guy. Welcome O welcome be thy glorious will,
thou great Archfactor of the Firmament.
O hadst thou let me lain but one day more,
to have reveal'd my self unto my Wife,
my dear, dear *Phillis*, who languisheth in pain,
hoping to see her aged Lord again.
Then had I been contented for to dye,
So am I now, thou must be pleas'd, not I.
Yet *Guy* bethink thee what thou hast to do,
wilt thou not make thy self known to thy Wife?
but thus unknown to any lose thy Life?
where no man ne're shall hear of thee at all,
nor give thy body Christian burial;
Yes, I will hye me strait to *Phillis* Gate,
and there reveal my self and my estate,
and my dear *Phillis*, whom I loved best,
shall close mine eyes, and bring my soul to rest.
But wilt thou break that vow of sanctity,
which thou didst make to him, that hath made thee;
and seek to contradict his holy will,
that hath shew'd such great mercies to thee still:
O God forbid! That vow true kept shall be,
I'le commit all to him that saved me.

            And

of Guy *Earl of* Warwick.

and when I dye, instead of Tomb or Grave,
I'le leave my body in my stone cold Cave.
Thither I will, and spend my short sweet dayes,
in contemplation and in holy prayers;
I poor old *Guy* go hye and hast thee thither,
for life and Pilgrimage must end together. *Exit.*

Enter Sparrow *Solus*.

Sparrow. Ha, ha, the world's well amended with me by-Lady, why? I am as plumb as a pudding now, for ever since I came to my young Master, I have been so puft up with good chear that Barly puddings are no meat, nor Cheese-cakes, nor Custards, no banquetting stuffe with me; for as soon as ever we came into *England*, my young Master goes to the Court presently, where he and I were Counterpain'd with such implements as passes; I am tost up and down like a Shittlecock in every bodies mouth; for who but Master *Sparrow*, the greatest Traveller that has been at cost twenty *Nobles* and *Jerico*, and I cannot tell ye where; but for all that I was serv'd a Sluttish trick to day, for my Master being bidden to a great Gentlemans house to dinner, took me along with him to wait at the Table; well as they were at Dinner, the Serving men as they took off the meat set it before the fire to keep it warm for themselves: I seeing the good chear standing in battle Ray, and having not broke my fast of all day, I began to draw near the fire, and look over my shoulder upon the victuals, at last I spyed a Fat legg of Pork; O how my Teeth did water to look upon't! I had not stood long, but seeing every body busie, I whipt the legg of Pork into my Pocket, and stood very mannerly with my hands at my back, as though I had done nothing; but it was not long, e're the Fat Pork with the heat of the Fire began to fry out of my Slops, & all the dogs in the House came Snukering and licking about my Breeches, and not content with that, but one unmannerly Cur above all the rest, popt his Nose into my Pocket, snatcht out the leg of Pork, & tore away all the tone side of my Breeches, that I was fain to go out edgling like a Crab isaith; put i'le ne're

F   steal

The Tragicall History

steal Pork again while I live, i'le have one bit of Mutton what-
some're comes on't ifaith.   *Exit Sparrow.*

Enter Guy *being in his Cave, to him the* Angell.

 Angell. Now *Guy* of *Warwick* is accomplished,
the full effect of all thy Pilgrimage,
then rise and pray, thy sins may be forgiven,
for Angels wait to bear thy soul to Heaven.   *Exit Angell.*   1420
 Guy. Gods will be done, I am resolv'd to dye,
and have askt mercy at the hands of him
that gave me Life, and now will take the same.
O what a pretious soul hath sinful man!
that in it self alone does comprehend
the figure, state, and lineaments of Heaven,
yet cannot measure nor define it self;
so when that all great workmen of the world,
had fram'd mans flesh out of a clod of clay,   1430
and all the Creatures of the Universal world,
of the same mould, to whom his very word
gave present life onely in mans brest,
that vil'd ambitious sinful heap of drosse;
he breathd his own breath, even the breath of heaven,
that is the glorious soul we now possesse,
which is immortal and can never dye.
Yet he that late was fram'd of mire and filth,
plac'd in a glorious state of innocence,
was not content, but striv'd to be as good   1440
as his great Maker, who could with one word,
throw him down headlong to the deepest Hell;
yet he in Mercy, Love, and meer good will,
did grant him pardon for his soul offence;
and seeing him unable to perform
his blessed will, did send his own dear Son
to pay his ransome with his precious blood,
and to redeem that soul which sinful man,
had forfeited to Satan, Death and Hell!;

            and

of Guy Earl of Warwick.

and for a death dam'd cursed and unpure,
he gave him life eternal to indure;
which life eternal, grant sweet Christ to me,
that in Heavens joyes I may thy glory see.
    Enter Rainborne and Herod of Arden with Sparrow.
 Rain. Go good Sir *Herod*, Post and meet the King,
who now is coming with his warlike Troops,
to meet my Father and to honour him,
in his return from fair *Jerusalem*.
 Herod. Hie you to *Warwick* Castle to your Mother,
tell her this happy news of his return,
whose absence long hath made her weep and mourn.
Come *Sparrow* you shall go along with me.
 Spar. Shall I go meet the King too Master?
 Rain. I Sir, you shall attend upon my friend.
 Spar. But I pray tell me one thing, is the King a Man or a Woman?
 Rain. He is a Man.
 Spar. Well, I shall never love him while I live; for a Cosin of his, the King of Clubs made me loose six pots of Ale, at Mother *Bunches* ifaith.
 Rainborne. Well Sir go along with him.
    Exit Sparrow and Herod.
Now *Rainborne* glut thy heart with wisht for joy,
O how it glads my soul, that I shall see,
my dear loved Father once before I dye!
The people flock together all on heaps,
Clapping their hands, aud crying out for joy,
that *Guy* of *Warwick* is come again,
and all report it of a certainty;
that in the dreadful day of *Winchester*,
he vanquisht *Colbron* in a single fight. *Guy groans.*
But stay, methinks I hear a doleful sound
of a departing man, and see here lies
an Aged Pilgrime, at the point of death;
what art thou Father? prethee speak to me:
 Guy. A poor age-withered Creature gentle Son,
that streight must yield my due unto my grave,

      F 2   for

The Tragicall History

for age and sicknesse now my life will have.
  Rain. Alas good Father thou art sick indeed,
yet if thou canst but lean upon my Arme,
I'le lead thee to a place where thou shalt be
comforted and attended carefully.
  Guy. I thank thee Son, but cannot leave this place;
yet if thy thoughts be equal with thy words,
let me request one kindnesse at thy hands,
it is the last that ever I shall make.
  Rain. Speak freely Father what soe're it be,
thy will shall be perform'd immediately.
  Guy. Then unto *Warwick* Castle hie thee straight,
enquire for *Phillis Guy* of *Warwicks* Wife,
deliver to her this same ring of Gold,
tell her an old poor Pilgrime at deaths dore,
did send it to her as a recompence,
for her good deeds, to him and many moe,
since her dear Lord away from her did go.
  Ramb. I'le give it her, as I have hope of Heaven,
and bring her with me hither presently;
that with sweet balmes she may comfort thee,
so fare thee well, sweet heaven thy comfort be.   *Exit.*
  Guy. Go on in peace, my peace with heaven is made,
thou goest to carry such a doleful gift,
as with the sight will kill my *Phillis* heart;
for when I took my leave to go from her,
that ring she gave me as a pledge of love;
which if I see quoth she, and thou not by,
Phillis will grieving weep, and weeping dye.
O did she know her *VVarwicks* death so nigh,
and he so ne're in a cold Cave to lye;
she soon would come and take her last adue
of him, whose love to her hath still been true;
but shall I dye before I see her face?
I feel death ceazing on my heart already;
O my sweet Saviour strengthen me this hour,
and in my weaknesse shew thy heavenly power.
I come, I come, to thee sweet Christ I flye,

save

of Guy *Earl of* Warwick.

save my poor soul, let my vile body dye. *He dies.*

Enter Phillis *and* Rainborne.

Phillis. O hast thee Son, and bring me to the man
that sent this Ring, alas we are undone!
it is thy Father Boy, good *Rainborne* run.
  Rain. You tell me wonders that amaze my soul,
it cannot be my Father that should lye,
in his own Country and his wife so nigh.
  Phillis. This is the Ring I gave him, which quoth he,
nothing but death shall ever part from me.
  Rain. See where he lies even yielding up the ghost.
  Phillis. If it be he, he hath a mould Wart underneath his
Ear.   *She looks under his Ear, and*
           cries out, they both kneel to him.
  Rain. View him good Mother, satisfie your mind.
  Phillis. It is my Husband, Oh my dearest Lord!
  Rain. O my dear Father speak unto thy Son,
but he is dead, and we are quite undone.
  Phillis. O gentle *Warwick*, speak one word to me,
I am thy wife that seven and twenty years
bewail'd thy absence even with woful Tears;
speak, speak, if any spark of life remains,
I'le think one look enough for all thy pains.
  Rain. See Mother now he looks upon us both,
and see how fast he holds my Fingers now;
something he wants, behold he maketh signes,
that we with our two hands should close his eyes.
Now it is done, see how he faints and dies.
  Phillis. O break my heart, that I with him may dye,
that in one grave our bodies both may lye.
  Rain. The King is coming, good mother be content;
O heavy is my heart, with too much grief is spent.

Enter Athelstone, Herod *with others.*

  Athelst. Sir *Herod* of *Arden* this is the time and place,
that I appointed for to meet Sir *Guy*,   and

The Tragicall History

and do him honour as he hath deserv'd,
but yet we have not heard where he remains.

Herod. See where Sir *Rainborne* and fair *Phillis* sits,
and in their Arms an aged Pilgrime lies.

Rain. And famous *Warwick* in this Pilgrime dies;
see mighty King, and worthy Lords behold
the flesh and blood of him, that when he lived,
was the most famous Knight that e're drew sword,
or clad his loins in compleat Arms of steel.

Athelst. O you have broke my heart with this sad news!
i'st possible my dearest friend Sir *Guy*,
should end his life, in such an uncouth place.
O cruel fate! O woful destiny!
arise fair Lady, sorrow helpeth not;
for if that sighs, or tears, could ought avail,
to bring his Heaven bred soul to Earth again;
my Kingly tears should day and night be spent,
to fetch it thence, but Heaven doth that prevent.

Rain. Your Tears, nor mine, dear Mother can prevail
nothing at all, Heaven hath appointed this,
Angells conduct his soul to endlesse blisse.

Athelst. *Rainborne* 'tis true, sweet *Phillis* weep no more,
lets comfort all our selves with thinking thus,
we must to him, but hee'l ne're come to us;
but in the honour of his worthy name,
the shield-bone of the bore of *Callidon*,
shall be hang'd up at *Civentries* great Gate;
the Ribs of the Dun Cow of *Dunsmore* Heath,
in *Warwick* Castle for a monument;
and on his Cave where he hath left his life,
a stately Hermitage I will erect,
in honour of Sir *Guy* of *Warwicks* Name;
passe mournfully along, wee'l follow all
his bloodlesse Corps, and heavy funeral.

Four takes the body of Guy, the rest follow.

Enter

of Guy Earl of Warwick.

Enter *Time* with the *Epilogue*.

THus Time *concludes this dolent History,*
And ends this Scene *with* GUY *of* Warwicks *Death* ;
So what is it but Time can bring to passe ?
Time *layes up Treasure where ther's Vertue scant,*
And gives the silly Fool when wise Men want :
Both Poor and Rich confesse my power Divine,
And every one doth say, make much of Time,
Through the whole World, while the world was, Time *rangeth,*
And 'tis mens manners, and not Time *that changeth.*
O you whose Souls look for Eternity,
Rest in the peace of perpetuity,
And kindly grant to this request of mine ;
For he's but young that writes of this Old Time.
Therefore if this your Eyes or Ears may please,
He means to shew you better things then these.   Exit *Time.*

Finis GUY of WARWICK.

---

of Guy Earl of Warwick.

Enter True with the Epilogue.

True Time, unfolder of delusive Errors,
Isat this Scene, with GUY of Warwicks Death;
So who but hee'd think our Story to bely'd?
Time layes up Troybers, nor the years for either so,
And opens the sly Door, where-wise Men went
Both Poor and Rich confute my power? Then lies
At last, I'm one daily I've made much of Time.
Wrongly done to deal with, while the works shun. Time ranges
And his own measures, and our Time short though the
Crown of his Child, to God Eternity.
While in the praise of Perpetuity
And heartily grant to thy renown of whites.
I'm the Debtor: the writer of this Old Times
It matters not how false or Fair it may chance
Be not too learn you better things than I do.

Exit Time.

Finis Guy of Warwick.